SWAN SANCTUARY'S GUIDE

TO RESPONSIBLE SWAN STEWARDSHIP

Educating one pond owner at a time

by
Lisbeth Ann Williams

Illustrations by Sandra Davis

DLD Books

Swan Sanctuary logo by Abby Wojtecki of Warrenton, VA

Cover photo: The author, loving her work

ISBN: 1514875853
ISBN–13: 978-1514875858

Written in gratitude to Dr. William J. L. Sladen

Nesting Swans

THIEF

A poem by Lisbeth Ann Williams

Fluidly she glides, her webbed feet propelling her
with graceful neck arched to head off the intruder.
Mate beside her swiftly, together to defend
outstretched wings glistening, the thief they apprehend.

Boy startled, clutching a creamy egg in each hand
feet tangled in weedy tendrils, struggling to stand.
He tries to flee, but from his hands the eggs escape
Like shooting stars, then sink into the inky lake.

Beneath the massive wings he cowers with head bent
while the swan relentlessly doles its punishment.
Snow white wings flashing in the late morning sun
foolish boy takes the blows for the deed he has done.

Trumpeting loudly, they at last cease their attack
with heads bobbing, to the nest they make their way back.
Thrusting her head into the straw where eggs had lain
in anguished lament the swan now searches in vain.

Heads submerged in bleak water, white tails upended
till the last rays of daylight with night are blended.
Nostrils still filled with the foul reek of human scent
she stops to preen, to rest, her energy now spent.

As night wraps itself around the sorrowful day
The swans feed quietly to chase hunger away.
Tucking her head beneath her wing, at last she sleeps
her faithful mate below, alert, the night watch keeps.

The swan upon her empty bed of straw still sits,
no eggs now will hatch into downy grey cygnets.
Not one egg in the carefully constructed nest
remains to be warmed beneath the swan mother's breast.

TABLE OF CONTENTS

As the question implies, anyone who is considering adding swans to their pond needs to give it thorough and extensive consideration. Swans are not pets, but wild animals, and this must be kept at the forefront of one's decision to acquire them.

This part of the book brings awareness to the reader regarding the problem of injured, old, convalescing or invasive swans that may be in need of a good home. It offers an alternative to buying swans off the illegal black markets that they have perhaps not thought of.

Most people do not realize or bother to investigate the important fact that swans are listed under the Migratory Bird Species Act with the U.S. Fish and Wildlife Service, and that having them requires a permit. Most state wildlife agencies require their own permit, in conjunction with the federal permit, in order to possess them. Once permits are obtained, the swans often require an identifying band or other means of identification.

Details the size, depth, water quality, and flora requirements necessary to the health and safety of swans.

Riparian buffers explained—what they are, why they are important, and specifics for creating them, as well as showing the detrimental effects of mowing all the way down to the pond edges. This chapter also emphasizes the importance of nearby wetland areas adjacent to ponds that may become homes for swans.

This section provides a detailed worksheet for determining whether or not a pond and the surrounding habitat are suitable for swans, and if not, what steps may be taken in order to provide for a swan's basic needs.

This is an in-depth worksheet for accessing the prevailing flora that are growing in and around a pond. It spans the three growing seasons in order to take into account the different peak bloom times.

This section emphasizes the crucial need for natural islands and/or rafts that provide safety for swans, as well as breeding areas. It includes a drawing of a simple wooden raft and instructions for anchoring it.

Swans rely on open water in order to feed, and this section addresses how to provide this most important safety measure during winter months. Step-by-step instructions show how to make a float for attaching a deicer and how to anchor it in the water.

Captive birds require supplemental feeding, especially during winter, when natural food supplies become depleted. This section focuses on types of feeders, how to mount them, and keeping them cleaned and sterilized.

This is a thorough list of materials and tools that should be on hand and available for swan owners who are responsible for captive swans.

When proper habitat is available, healthy adult swans are rarely prone to predation; however, in captivity, where habitat is unsafe, or if a swan is injured or ill, this can be a problem. Young cygnets are the most vulnerable and are often victims of snapping turtles. This section provides important ways to keep swans safe.

Swans that are not wild and unable to fly are often transported from one pond to another, or to veterinarians in the case of emergencies. They are susceptible to foot injuries, so the focus here is on how they can be transported in a safe manner, keeping stress to a minimum.

Lead poisoning and electrocution by power lines are the biggest threats to swans. Automobiles also become a danger when swans that have been rendered flightless attempt to move about in areas that are not fenced. Being aware of these potential dangers and taking steps to minimize them will ensure the safety of swans.

Emergencies are never planned for, often come at the least opportune times, and also cause turmoil and increased stress when they are not prepared for in advance. This chapter provides an emergency backup plan and strongly advocates swan emergency preparedness.

Dry pens are small, temporary pens built on land that provide a safe place to keep a swan for a short period of time: for relocating the swan to another pond, separating parents from cygnets for pinioning or banding, separating aggressive swans, or keeping one that is ill. I provide a detailed description of the materials needed and how to build one.

The wet pen is very similar to the dry pen, but part or most of it is in the water. It is somewhat more challenging to build than the dry pen, but it is also used more frequently than the dry pen because swans need to be near water. Instructions on how to build the pen are included, along with suggestions for making it predator-proof.

Prior to being placed in a pen or kennel for transporting, swans need to be caught. Occasionally, an injured or sick bird can be run down and caught by hand or with a net, but most of the time, trapping is a well-thought-out and time-consuming process. There are several types of traps that can be used, and this chapter provides instructions for building them.

This chapter details the steps to be taken prior to actual trapping and elaborates on the procedures involved in this process, including the necessary equipment.

PREFACE

I began writing this book with some trepidation, because I do not believe that swans or any bird should ever be held captive. Still, for centuries, man has imposed his own will on those species with which we share this planet. Those with wings have an inherent right to fly. It is undeniably wrong to believe that we have the authority to take this innate ability from them and to so shamefully diminish their grace and beauty. Flying is the means by which birds can escape predators. In rendering them flightless by either pinioning or feather clipping them, we put them at risk, and we greatly inhibit their ability to find adequate nutrition. Ultimately, however, it is through understanding that we can overcome ignorance. If, in reading this book, the reader gains understanding, then it will not have been written in vain.

In essence, the purpose of this book is twofold. The first goal is to educate. I would like to educate the public, one pond owner at a time, about the importance of protecting our two native swan species, while discouraging the illegal proliferation of the non-native Mute Swan. Good swan stewardship calls for understanding their behavior, their food and habitat requirements, and the federal and local laws as they pertain to their management. For those who have proper habitat and the desire to care for swans, this book will arm you with the knowledge and the resources to do so responsibly.

My second goal is to inform potential swan owners about Swan Sanctuary, which I began in 2010. It provides a haven for birds that may not be able to survive on their own due to pinioning, injury or age to live out their lives in relative safety and in a hospitable environment. It provides an alternative in which Mute Swans, considered invasive by the U.S. Fish and Wildlife Service and most state wildlife agencies, can live celibate lives as non–breeders while adding enjoyment to the lives of those who wish to care for them.

Swan Sanctuary maintains a list of pond owners who meet requirements for pond habitat. It serves as a liaison between swans and pond owners, providing birds for adoption as they become available. Through its interaction with the public, Swan Sanctuary helps raise public awareness about our native Trumpeter and Tundra Swans and the dangers that threaten their survival. It also provides assistance to pond owners seeking to improve and naturalize their wetlands and pond habitat—not only for the health and survival of swans, but also for a multitude of waterfowl and other aquatic species.

It is my sincerest hope that this book will become the primary source of information for potential pond owners to turn to, and that it will awaken in them a desire to protect swans and their habitats for future generations.

INTRODUCTION

This book is a compilation of first-hand experiences accumulated while caring for a large swan collection in Warrenton, Virginia. The collection comprised mainly Trumpeter Swans and their descendants, those birds remaining from the original Trumpeter Swan Migration Project, which sought to teach the Trumpeter Swan a migration route using an ultra-light airplane. This was inspired by a similar undertaking with Canada geese, which had proved quite successful. The movie *Fly Away Home*, though fictional, was based on that endeavor.

The swan project, which began in 2000 at Airlie, in Virginia, and ended in 2003, was headed up by Gavin G. Shire and Dr. William J. L. Sladen. A detailed summary of this project may be found in *Ultra Swan Project*, by Elinor Osborn. The study ended after the third year. It had been costly, dangerous, and disappointing. Following the ultra-light project, the Swan Research Program remained under the umbrella of the larger entity, Environmental Studies on the Piedmont, in Warrenton, Virginia.

When I arrived in 2004, I began volunteering and helping to care for the swans that had been retired from the ultra-light experiment, as well as some of their offspring and hybrids from later studies. I often consulted the swan data that had been collected, as it contained information on each and every swan from the original ultra–light experiment, as well as their progeny. Most of the information I provide in this book is taken from my own direct experience, which came from years of working with the swan collection at Airlie. (Airlie is an exclusive conference center that boasts nine ponds and mitigation areas amidst a natural setting.)

Dr. Sladen is now retired as director of the Swan Research Program; however, as Director Emeritus, he continues to be a vast reservoir of knowledge for those who care to consult with him. Unfortunately, no new studies have ensued under the new directorship. Bill Sladen has been my chief advisor and mentor over the years. I am indebted to him for the knowledge he so generously shared and for his help in ensuring the accuracy of the botany in the Wetland Habitat Assessment included in Chapter III of this book.

I am a firm believer that we each come into this life with a purpose, or Dharma, to fulfill. Some are fortunate enough to have a clear vision at a young age and thus begin to chart their course for a future that will bring their sketchy dreams into full living color. Others trip and stumble along their journey and take a side trip or two before they finally set their sail, turning away from the distractions which may have led them off course earlier in life. When looking back over the previous decades, we often find that every turn in the road helped to prepare us for the events in front of us. I was one of those who plodded along in my life, often uncertain and unclear, yet always feeling a gentle nudge urging me forward to embrace the necessary risks required to fulfill my dreams.

When I was four, I lived with my grandmother and her husband in the Rocky Mountains of Colorado. This was a happy, but very brief, period of my childhood. I was given a duck for Easter, with whom I fell in love. He followed me everywhere, of course, due to the imprinting that we now know causes waterfowl to attach themselves to the first other that they see in their lives. A short time later, much to my dismay, my mother retrieved me and I was taken back to grow up in the suburbs, minus my beloved duck.

During the subsequent years, every weekend in the summer, I was packed up with my siblings and a boat and taken to a reservoir, where my mother insisted that I learn to water ski. I did not take to the competitive aspect of this sport, as my mother pushed me to. Still, there was something about being in the watery environment and playing in the lake, with its squishy, muddy bottom, that touched something deep within me. It was not until many years later, after my own children were grown, that I would be able to return to a reservoir with an entirely different focus from water skiing.

I fell in love with gardening while I was raising my daughters as a single mom in the '80s and '90s. Water gardens were becoming popular then, and one day I opened up a newspaper, which is something I rarely did, to an article about a local park that had brought in a pair of black swans to reside there. I suddenly knew that I wanted a pond *and I wanted swans!* This was one of those serendipitous events that remind us that there is a greater intelligence guiding us to where we need to be.

Finally, my last daughter had fledged, and I was free to pursue my own life anew. I sold my home in the Denver suburbs and left in search of property with a pond in the country. I had been checking out books from the library and reading up on swans. I was focused for a while, but amid the uncertainty of being uprooted from my former life, I was convinced that property on top of a mountain in Tennessee was the thing to buy. I was assured that I could always make a pond. This turned out to be a terrible mistake, and three years later, I found myself in Warrenton, Virginia. I purchased a small house in town, and I gave up my dream of having swans. This was surely Divine Guidance, however, because a few months after moving there, I discovered Airlie and The Swan Research Program, less than two miles from where I was living! They were in need of volunteers, and I wasted no time in offering to do all that they would allow me to do.

During those months, I felt more joy than I had ever known. I was helping with observations and feeding the collection of about 90 swans. Later that year, I had the opportunity to spend a week in England. Bill Sladen, a British native, had connections at the Welney Wildfowl & Wetlands Trust, so I was given the privilege of feeding the Whooper and Bewick's Swans during my visit. When the Swan Research Program decided to raise cygnets in an incubator, I was allowed to be the number one surrogate mom in charge of their care. This was greater bliss than I had ever imagined possible. I do not know the author of the most apropos description, that "I would light up like a Christmas tree" whenever I began to talk about the swans. They had become the most important thing in my life, and the word "passion" does not even begin to describe how I felt about them.

I would like to say that things went well from then on, but pangs of guilt and doubt haunted me. My daughters were raising children of their own by that time, and I was missing them, along with the grandchildren I barely knew. Once again, I had lost my way on my soul's journey. I returned to Denver, but I was miserable there. Too many years had passed for me to resume my former profession. I began to contemplate the idea of creating a swan sanctuary, although I did not have a clue how to go about it. Eventually, I returned to Virginia and to the Swan Research Program.

Many changes had taken place in my absence. Dr. Sladen had retired, and Brooke Pennypacker, who had been in charge of the ultra–light and the swans, had left. A biologist, John Whissel, had been hired in his place, while a younger biologist, Sean Campbell, and a female assistant had been hired to carry on the care of the collection. I asked them if they needed any help, and I was once again put in charge of feeding.

I continued to volunteer for the next three and a half years, taking every opportunity to be more involved and to learn everything that I possibly could in the process. I regretted having left earlier, thinking that had I remained, I might have been offered a permanent position. I longed from the depths of my soul to become an integral part of the Swan Research Program. Sean was an excellent teacher and had incredible patience with me. He asked me to assist him more frequently.

I was able to move into a rental house located literally at the back door of Airlie. This was ideal, because I was able to tend to sick and injured birds sometimes twice a day, and even more frequently when necessary. My proximity to the swans was a great help to the biologists who did not live nearby. I was invited to attend the regular meetings with Dr. Sladen, who was now acting as Director Emeritus for the larger entity, Environmental Studies on the Piedmont.

More changes were taking place within the institution. The Swan Research Program was attempting to separate from Environmental Studies and stand alone as a 501(c)(3), but not without great resistance. The issue came to a head in 2009, when the female assistant was let go. Soon after, John Whissel reached an impasse with the new director and left as well. Now only Sean and I were left to take care of the collection, which had decreased from more than 90 to only about 70 swans. Sean and I worked well together and things went smoothly. I became the scribe for our weekly meetings with Dr. Sladen, and I was grateful to have reached this place in my life. I had a dream, however, of beginning a swan sanctuary, and I had begun to look for property to buy, with a pond. On Thanksgiving of 2009, I found that property. I was able to purchase this property with my husband at the time and moved in during the spring of 2010. At last I would have swans of my own!

Then, much to my surprise, about six months later, Sean left the program abruptly. The split between Environmental Studies and The Swan Research Program had still not come about, so technically, the swans were owned by Environmental Studies. The current director and his staff were in a quandary, so they offered me the position of contractor/consultant to look after the swan collection. I was ecstatic. My long–held desire to become an integral part of the swan program had at last come true. This kick–started Swan Sanctuary into a reality, since I was working as a contractor and not as an employee.

Thus began a very challenging and satisfying conclusion to my hard work and efforts. I had to teach myself so many things that Sean had not gotten around to showing me. I consulted old data in the office and Bill Sladen, and I managed to care for the collection, for the most part single–handedly. When I occasionally needed help, I had to rely on volunteers. They were often not available or lived too far out, so I learned to manage alone most of the time. Fortunately, the Sladens' longtime assistant, H. T. Anderson, who had experience with the swans, helped me on numerous occasions. It was hard, very physical work at times, and I worked in all kinds of weather. But I was living my bliss, and all was right with the world, because I was doing what I loved. What was most important was that I was doing something that would one day make a difference.

If this sounds like a fairy tale, perhaps it was. In truth, life goes on and change is constant. In my happiness, I apparently did not notice that my husband was not happily supporting me in what I was doing. In fact, he cared nothing at all for the swans, which were the love of my life. The life I had worked so hard to build suddenly came tumbling down when he abandoned our marriage of 15 years. The financial devastation that followed forced me to sell my property. Not knowing what else to do amid confusion and financial ruin, I once again found myself leaving the swans behind and returning to Colorado.

The new director had brought in another person, whom he expected me to train in less than two weeks. I was aghast that he thought this person could learn in a matter of a few *hours* what had taken me *years* to learn. The woman that I was to train did not even know that more than one species of swans existed! I knew she was totally inadequate to take over the position, and she showed little actual interest in the swans. I believe she was merely using the director to aid her in reaching her own personal goals.

The director himself had limited knowledge of the swans, and the ongoing feud between him and Dr. Sladen prevented him from seeking Dr. Sladen's expertise. The over-inflated egos and backstabbing among professors was foreign to me, and I could not understand how they could let this stand in the way of the well-being of the swans. I felt sick about leaving the swans that I had come to know personally and had cared for, but it was now out of my hands.

As I prepared to write down some notes for my replacement, I realized that there was far too much information, and that the years I had spent gaining my experience could not simply be summarized in a couple of pages. It was at this point that I knew I needed to write a book to help preserve some of the work begun by Dr. Sladen. I am honored to have known him and to be considered his friend. This book is written partially in tribute to him—and, of course, to the swans themselves.

Proceeds from the sale of this book will help with the finances needed to get Swan Sanctuary back on its feet. Although at the writing of this book, the sanctuary is in a holding pattern, I am determined to see it re–birthed and functioning as an indispensable entity for the future of swans. I know that there is a need not only to help the swans, but to educate the general public. This can be done through Swan Sanctuary, one pond owner at a time!

CHAPTER I

THE GREAT AMBASSADORS

Why Keep Swans?

The first and most obvious reason for keeping swans is for their elegance and beauty. But there are other reasons for having swans that benefit the swans themselves, rather than merely to satisfy our human desire to acquire pets and objects.

Dr. Bill Sladen, founder of the North American Waterfowl Trust in Maryland and the Swan Research Program at Airlie in Warrenton, Virginia, referred to the Trumpeter Swans as "wetland ambassadors." In addition to the splendor that they add to any pond, swans are beneficial to the health of your pond. The submerged aquatic vegetation, or SAV, provides the bulk of a swan's diet. These are the plants growing underwater, often cursed and chemically controlled by uninformed pond owners. The swans' long necks provide them the ability to pull these plants up from a depth of 3' to 4'. This is why you often see a swan upended, with only its bottom and webbed feet waving above the water's surface. They are feeding along the pond floor and will often remain with their heads underwater, popping up for only an occasional breath of air. They also feed on small crustaceans and snails, which add protein to their diet.

When proper habitat is maintained around a pond by allowing the SAV to grow and by allowing a riparian buffer to grow up around the pond, it will attract other wetland species. Having an island or a raft in the pond provides added appeal, because it provides swans and other birds a safe place to escape predators, especially at night and when the pond becomes partially or completely frozen during winter. With proper habitat, you will probably also have great blue herons, green herons, red–winged blackbirds, tree swallows, Canada geese, kingfishers, several duck species, and possibly even the great white egret.

Some people do not like having Canada geese around, because they believe that they are messy. If you have habitat that is attractive to swans, it is actually less attractive to the geese. Geese prefer feeding on short, mowed grass, so if you let a buffer grow up around your pond, the geese will be deterred. They do not like to cross this barrier.

Perhaps you have a dream of owning property with a lake or a pond. Perhaps you already have property and a pond, and you are contemplating how nice it would be to see a pair of swans swimming on it. You may have even looked on the Internet to see where you might purchase a pair, or perhaps you have already purchased them. If you obtained young birds, chances are they have already been pinioned (rendered flightless) to ensure that they will stay on your pond. Pinioning is a way of protecting your investment as well as complying with state and federal laws. You may have paid upwards of $1,000 per bird. Your swans may wish to fly off in search of greener pastures and bluer waters, but if they cannot fly, they will be inhibited from doing this. They can, of course, walk off your property if it is not fenced, which puts their lives in jeopardy.

It is not uncommon for people of sufficient financial means to make such a purchase without bothering to research and consider the implications of such a decision. Swan stewardship is a serious commitment. It is my sincerest hope that this book, along with my website, http://www.swansanctuary.org, will arm you with the knowledge and means by which you may provide excellent habitat and superior care for your swans.

Few people are aware that there are seven different species of swans, only two of which are indigenous to North America. Many swans are purchased off the black market, and most of those are Mute Swans, which have been declared illegal to own in most states. In places along the Eastern and the Western Seaboard, the Mute Swan is now routinely euthanized or killed. In fact, the federal government has implemented a policy making it illegal to have, buy, or sell Mute Swans.

If you have a pond and you are still deliberating whether or not you wish to become the guardian for captive swans, there are many factors to consider. First of all, you must consider the size of the pond and determine if it is adequate for the species you want to have. A pair of Trumpeter Swans requires a pond of an acre or more in size to ensure that they will have a sufficient source of food and also to provide adequate space. Swans are territorial, especially during the breeding season.

Breeding Pairs versus Rescue Birds

If your heart is set on having a pair of swans, and they have reached breeding age of three to four years, you must realize that *each and every* spring, they will begin to prepare their nest. They will lay eggs. The pen (the female) will incubate the eggs, and the cob (the male) will defend the territory. In about 30 days, the eggs will hatch, if they have not been eaten by snapping turtles or other predators. Your heart will leap with delight when you see the proud parents swimming around your pond with cygnets in tow. Mute Swans are especially endearing, as they often carry the young on their backs, tucked safely within the protection of the mother's wings.

In a captive situation, swans are generally pinioned or feather clipped. Pinioning is permanent and will render the bird flightless for the duration of its life. Wing clipping or feather clipping is a temporary condition imposed to achieve the same result as pinioning; however, because it is not permanent, it requires a repeat performance each year after the molt.

If you are planning to pinion cygnets, they must be caught at about two to three weeks of age. You will need to separate them from the parents for a short time while you complete the task, which should be done by someone who is experienced. Once the bleeding has been checked, you can immediately return them to the parents and to the pond. If you wait beyond three weeks to pinion, they will need to be caught and transported to an avian veterinarian. Pinioning is more dangerous at the juvenile to adult age and far more stressful to the bird at that time, not to mention more costly. Even with an older swan, it is far better for the bird if you can find a vet who is willing to travel to your location to do the pinioning. The swans can be released back into the water immediately, or at least within 24 hours, thus greatly minimizing their stress.

Over the next couple of months, both parents will molt their flight feathers and grow new ones. During this time, they will be flightless. When the new feathers grow in, the natural instinct is for the parents to begin giving flight lessons to their young, which should by now have also grown flight feathers. This is where you must seriously consider your role as landlord and what your permits will or will not allow you to do. If the parents are pinioned, they will not have the ability to teach their young to fly. If the juveniles have not already been pinioned, they will probably eventually figure out flying on their own. The juveniles will remain with the parents for the first year, but very often, when the following spring comes around, the parents will kick them out. In the wild, the juveniles will join with juveniles from other pairs and other non–breeders, forming social groups.

However, in a captive situation, if the cygnets have been pinioned and there are no other juveniles or adults to whom they may attach themselves, you will need to decide what to do with them. Occasionally you will have a pair that does not mind the juveniles being in close proximity, but if this is not the case, you will need to find new homes for them. This is where it can get complicated.

If the cygnets are Mute Swans, it is now illegal to possess, buy, or sell them. In the case of Mute Swans, the wise thing is to (1) destroy the nest to prevent nesting, (2) remove the eggs from the nest, or (3) addle or oil the eggs to prevent their hatching. You can eat any eggs that you remove from the nest so long as it is done promptly after the egg is laid. The mother swan may continue to lay more eggs; however, this puts more stress on her body. Addling must be done at the proper stage and the eggs then removed after a few weeks' time, or the mother may continue to incubate, which will cause her to lose weight and suffer diminished health. Instructions for correctly addling eggs may be found in Chapter VII. If you are raising Black Swans or Black–Necked Swans, you will need to check with your state and your permits to see what is allowed. Also, Black Swans, unlike native species that breed only in the spring, will breed at any time of year.

If you are determined to raise cygnets and realize the commitment and energy involved—and, most importantly, realize that the swans will breed every year like clockwork—then you will want to consider keeping a healthy pair of Trumpeters. There are reintroduction programs seeking juveniles and sexually mature, mated pairs to help in their reestablishment. Please also consider becoming a member of The Trumpeter Swan Society to help support this effort.

Permits

Because all swans have been lumped under the Migratory Bird Species Act with the U.S. Fish and Wildlife Service, you will need to apply for a permit enabling you to possess, buy, and sell the birds. You will not be able to obtain a permit for a Mute Swan, because it has been placed on the invasive species list and many states have ordered them to be killed. I will talk more about this species in Chapter II. Since most state agencies work in conjunction with the federal ones, you will most likely be required to have a state permit, as well, depending on where you live. There are non-refundable fees required when you apply for a permit, and it can take several weeks to several months to obtain approval.

The next thing you must consider is whether or not you plan to have the swans pinioned or feather clipped. Your permits may require you to do one or the other. They may also require you to mark them with identifying tarsus and/or neckbands. Pinioning is a means by which the swan is made permanently flightless, by removing the flight feathers at the joint of one or both wings.

This is not noticeable when the swan is at rest, but is easily seen when the swan stretches its wings. The reason for rendering a bird flightless is to prevent it from flying away in search of a place more to its liking. The important thing to remember is that once you have imposed this condition on your swan, you then become 100 percent responsible for its care. This means that you must provide supplemental feeding at certain times of the year, since the swan will no longer be able to seek out its own food sources. Depending on where you live, your pond will become depleted in winter, when natural food sources stop growing.

Pinioning is usually done at about two to three weeks of age with a fingernail clipper. Once the bleeding has stopped, the cygnet is returned to its parents and suffers minimal trauma. Pinioning may also be achieved with an adult swan, but it must be done by a veterinarian who specializes in avian care. The wound will be sutured and bandaged, and an antibiotic will usually be administered. The bird must be kept confined and out of water for at least 24 hours. The veterinarian may tell you to keep it out of water for two weeks, but I have found this to be excessive and unnecessary. The birds are wild, not domestic like your dog or cat, and therefore will heal and begin eating again when stress is kept to a minimum and they are returned to their familiar environment.

There is another procedure known as a tenectomy. This is far more complicated and requires that the bird be bandaged and kept confined for six to eight weeks. I view this particular method as nothing short of torture and do not recommend it under any circumstances.

There is a period of about a month when the bird is naturally flightless due to the annual molt. This is when the old flight feathers are shed and new ones are grown. A non-permanent method of maintaining flightlessness is by yearly feather clipping, after the molt has been completed. This requires diligence on the part of the owner. Not all birds molt at the same time, and poor health can affect the timing of the molt. If a pair is raising a brood of cygnets, generally the parents will not molt at the same time. The pen usually begins to shed her feathers first, while the cob retains his until her new ones have grown in. This allows him to protect his mate and the cygnets until their new feathers have grown in.

Molting always occurs in the very late spring to early summer, after nesting season. In the case of a nesting female, it will not occur until after her cygnets have hatched—probably late June to late July. This way, her new flight feathers are growing in while her cygnets' feathers are also growing. When flight feathers of both the mother and the cygnets have grown in sufficiently, she and her mate will begin giving flight lessons to their cygnets, which are now considered juveniles. For those birds that are migratory, it is vital to their survival, to build up their strength, as well as the ability to fly in order to make the long journey to their wintering grounds.

If feather clipping is done before the new feathers have hardened, they may bleed. This means that you must wait and recapture the bird in a few weeks' time. If you wait too long, the birds may fly off before you can get them feather clipped. This involves time and work. Traps must be set up to capture the birds, and at least one other person needs to assist in the operation. This is also the time to examine the birds for any health issues, get their weight, and check the condition of any neck or tarsus bands that they may already have. If you are trapping a new family and you are marking the juveniles with numbered bands, feather clipping or pinioning is often done at the same time.

Of course, a much simpler way to enjoy swans on your pond is to create enticing habitat that will attract wild ones to stop in. If they like what you have to offer, they may spend the winter there and return year after year, with juveniles in tow. If you live in an area along the East or West coasts, within range of the Tundra Swan migration path from Alaska, you may see them flying through. This requires no permit, and you can simply enjoy observing them.

The Swan Species

Trumpeter Swan
(Cygnus buccinator)

Tundra Swan
(Cygnus columbianus)

Bewick's Swan
(Cygnus bewickii)

Whooper Swan
(Cygnus cygnus cygnus)

Mute Swan
(Cygnus olor)

Black-Necked Swan
(Cygnus melancoryphus)

Black Swan
(Cygnus atratus)

CHAPTER II

THE SPECIES

Several books have been written devoted to descriptions and habits of the swan species. I am including this information as well, because if you want to have swans, it is best to be armed with as much knowledge as possible.

Swans are classified under the phylum Chordata (having a backbone), class Aves (avian), order Anseriformes, family Anatidae. The genus is Cygnus (swan). There are seven to nine species of swans, depending upon which expert you wish to agree with. The Coscoroba Swan and the snow goose are two species that have not been clearly agreed upon. Only two species are native to North America: the Trumpeter and the Tundra Swans. The Mute Swan is an introduced species of Eurasian descent. If you have grown up on either of the two coasts or in the northern central states, you have probably seen the Tundra Swan, formerly known as the Whistling Swan, and possibly, on rarer occasions, caught a glimpse of the magnificent Trumpeter Swan. If you live in the southern or lower states, you may never have had the opportunity to see a swan other than at a private zoo or a park. In these settings, you will most likely see Mute

Swans and occasionally the Black Swan and the Black–Necked Swan. My only regret is that I cannot provide for you in this book the wonderful vocalizations of these birds or the sound of their wings when they are flying in for a landing. To witness this first hand is truly a gift.

The Trumpeter Swan had nearly disappeared in the early 1900s, but some of the restoration efforts have seen some success. It is possible that some of the Trumpeters are once again learning migration routes from the Tundra Swans and may occasionally be seen with the Tundra Swans in winter.

Tundra Swan (Cygnus columbianus)

Nothing can compare to the sound of the Tundra Swans on their migration south for the winter! They are the most abundant swan in North America. The Tundra Swan was previously known as the Whistling Swan due to its vibrant song, which is carried on the wind during flight. It is smaller than the Trumpeter Swan and usually has a uniquely sized and shaped yellow lore just below the eye, which can serve as an identifying mark. (The lore is the region between the eye and bill on the side of a bird's head.) The bill is not as straight as that of the Trumpeter, having an ever so slight upward tilt. It carries its body differently, too. When vocalizing, the Tundra leans out and stretches its neck forward. This always reminds me of The Teapot Song (I'm a Little Teapot). It was written by George Harold Sanders and Clarence Z. Kelley and published in 1939.

I'm a little teapot, short and stout.
Here is my handle, here is my spout.
When I get all steamed up,
I just shout.
Tip me over and pour me out!

Tundra Swans are generally seen in large flocks and often feeding in farmers' fields. Breeding pairs spend their summers nesting on the tundra in Alaska and parts of Canada. The nests are bowl–shaped and usually situated on a mound or ridge. They are built from grasses and sedges and lined with lichens, moss, and down from the mother's breast. Tundra Swans will defend their nests from smaller predators but often abandon them at the approach of a human, wolf, or bear in order to draw them away from the nest. They have a varied diet consisting of aquatic and sub–aquatic vegetation, seeds, tubers, grains, mollusks, and arthropods.

The largest groups migrate south along the Pacific coast to spend the winter, while a smaller population migrates across parts of Canada and the northern United States, and also along the Atlantic as far south as North Carolina. Theirs is one of the longest migrations of any bird—nearly 2,000 miles! In winter you will find them in shallow lakes, ponds, rivers, and estuaries if they have survived the hunting season. There are state organizations that receive huge donations from hunting organizations (which I will not name) in order to have control over the waterfowl at large. There is an Atlantic Flyway Council, a Mississippi Flyway Council, a Central Flyway Council, and a Pacific Flyway Council. These oversee migrating bird populations and manage hunting practices pertaining to the welfare of each species. Unfortunately, hunting of Tundra Swans is allowed in several states. That would not seem so bad if the hunter wanted one to feed his family, but sadly, most hunting that is done these days is merely to acquire a trophy.

Trumpeter Swan (Cygnus buccinator)

The Trumpeter Swan was nearly made extinct, and was in fact thought to be extinct, until a small, non-migratory group was found in the Yellowstone area. Prior to the early 1900s, they were hunted mainly for their feathers to adorn women's hats, and also because their feathers made the best quill pens. This led to a rapid decline in their numbers. Thanks to organizations like The Trumpeter Swan Society, The Wyoming Wetlands Society, and other dedicated reintroduction programs, their numbers are increasing.

Migration routes are passed along by the parents to their offspring. Many of the newer populations have lost this knowledge and consequently are non-migratory. However, there is evidence that new routes are being forged and their territories are expanding. I have personally witnessed a few Trumpeter Swans flying in with Tundra Swans to spend the winter at Airlie, in Virginia. I believe that with enough concerned individuals and diligent monitoring, this phenomenon will increase. There is nothing that can compare to the breathtaking sound of Trumpeter Swans flying in for a landing on their fluid airstrip.

Trumpeters are the largest of the North American swans. They swim with necks tall and erect. Their bills are completely black and straight. It is no wonder that the swan has been considered sacred throughout history and has been one of the most beloved of animals for millennia. To many Native American tribes, such as the Lakota, the Trumpeter is a symbol of grace, healing, and knowledge.

The Trumpeters breed in freshwater lakes, ponds, and marshes and build their nests on islands. If an island is not available, they will build on top of a beaver lodge or a muskrat mound. The eggs are laid every other day. Once they have all been laid, the pen will incubate them for approximately 34 days.

There was one Trumpeter at Airlie that built her nest near the water's edge. When her eggs failed to hatch, she continued to sit on the nest, where she was later predated. This, I believe, was due to overcrowding and the lack of suitable nest sites.

Trumpeters generally lay between one and eight eggs. The most that I have seen hatch successfully is seven. It appears that a more experienced mother lays more eggs than one who is new at breeding.

The young cygnets have soft, gray down and pink feet and bills. As juveniles, they are a mottled gray with pinkish feet and bills. They finally begin to resemble the parents at maturity—about one year. They will begin to form pair bonds at age three or four and generally mate for life.

They spend the winters in reservoirs, lakes, streams, and ponds. Their diet consists primarily of sub–emergent aquatic vegetation when it is available, along with small crustaceans that are pulled up with the plants. They also eat various grasses, grains, and berries, such as pokeberries. The cygnets feed on duckweed, lichen, and mosses growing on the pond surface. When fully grown, a female Trumpeter can weigh from 20 to 25 pounds (9 to 12 kilograms), while the male can weigh anywhere from 21 to 38 pounds (9.5 to 17 kilograms). The life span for swans can range between 20 and 30 years.

Mute Swan (Cygnus olor)

The Mute Swan, being non–migratory, is semi–domesticated. I have found it to be far gentler and sweeter in nature than our wilder Tundra and Trumpeter Swans. It is the swan most often seen gracing parks and zoos and depicted in art. Easily recognized by its protruding knob and red–orange bill, the Mute Swan is about the same size as the Trumpeter and the Whooper Swan. There is also a Polish Mute, which displays a very pale orange bill and beige, rather than black, feet. The Mute Swan makes a kind of snorting sound, not unlike a horse, so the implication that it is mute is not truly accurate. It is, however, far quieter than the Trumpeter and the Tundra Swans. It is very graceful and often glides with its wings held high over its back. It carries its young in this small protected area when they are very small. It also adopts this posture to show aggression.

Although they are not migratory, there are still some Mute Swans flying around that occasionally turn up in people's ponds. I believe that, as with any other bird, if we provide what they need, they will come on their own, and if they find a hospitable environment, they will keep coming back and may even decide to stay and raise a family.

Sadly, many of today's privately owned swans were purchased on the black market. Mute Swans are typically sold to misguided pond owners. People love to see the cygnets led around by their protective parents, but seldom do they consider the complications that arise in our modern world as a result of yearly reproduction.

The Mute Swan has endured undeserved criticism in recent years. As the story goes, there was a captive pair of Mute Swans that escaped during a hurricane and began to breed prolifically. The swan has been unfairly accused of those wrongs that have been fully and completely caused by human ignorance and human arrogance.

The Mute Swan is revered in England, where all are owned by the Queen, but in North America it has become the scapegoat for many of the environmental issues confronting the

Chesapeake Bay on the East Coast. The powers that be claim that the Mute Swan is solely responsible for habitat destruction and for depleting the food sources needed by our migrating native Tundra Swans. The U.S. Fish and Wildlife Service has pronounced it to be an invasive species and many states have followed suit.

Reduced to nuisance status, thousands of Mute Swans have been slaughtered and euthanized. When I first began volunteering for the Swan Research Program, I believed all this, because this is what I heard from the biologists in charge of the program. I have since done some research of my own, and I have discovered a great political agenda behind these questionable accusations. As I delved further, I began to see that agriculture practices, pig farms, and sewage treatment plants are by far the greatest detriment to these water systems and ecology, although the Mute Swan receives the brunt of the blame.

So, although the Mute Swan has been classified as invasive, I believe it is unethical and immoral to kill them. There are other agencies—and that includes me—who find it more humane to adopt the Mute Swans either as single, celibate birds or as same-sex couples. This works all right as long as you have two female Mutes; however, I have found that if you put two males together, they will end up fighting and one will usually be injured. If you are seriously considering adding swans to your pond, please consider taking in one that is less fortunate, rather than a breeding pair.

I have heard the Mute Swan criticized (and also the Canada goose) for attacking while protecting its territory, its nest, and its young. I find this absurd, because what mother in her right mind would *not* protect her young if she felt threatened?

In the spring of 2012, I was contacted by a major television station because a man had been drowned by a Mute Swan. Only hours before receiving the call, I had been out alone in a boat checking one of our own Mute Swan nests. I can only surmise that this person did not take the proper precautions and more than likely drowned because of his own carelessness. The news woman who had contacted me wanted instant gratification for her sensational story, which she planned to air the following morning. I told her that I was busy and would have to get back with her in a couple of hours, but when I tried to call her back, she was unavailable. I was grateful that my name was not associated with the negative publicity that was portrayed in her newscast. This was just one more incident that served to kindle injustice perpetrated by those who already have a vendetta against the Mute Swan.

Whooper Swan (Cygnus cygnus)

The Whooper Swan is the Eurasian version of our Trumpeter Swan. It is similar in size, but a large portion of its bill is yellow. Its call is loud and joyful and of a higher pitch than that of the Trumpeter Swan.

During my 2004 visit to the Welney Wildfowl & Wetlands Trust in England, I had the privilege of feeding the Whooper and the Bewick's Swans on their daily evening visit to the park. The loud chorus of their arrival at dusk was something I will never forget. While I was accustomed to feeding the swans at Airlie by filling feeders that were placed in the water at a depth of about 3', the swans at Welney were fed by an attendant walking along the shore with a wheelbarrow full of corn and tossing out scoops in all directions for the hungry birds. This was done just below a blind, where observers could sit and witness them in the wild with binoculars and telescopes. It was a truly memorable experience.

During my many years of caring for the swans at Airlie, we had two Whooper Swans in our collection of mostly Trumpeters. Even if I did not see them, I could usually locate them simply by their energetic vocalization. The older male, who was the father of the female, was the oldest swan we had, and he died at the age of 22. Sadly, both of the Whoopers were loners, and though they were tolerated by the other swans, they were never accepted as part of the group.

Bewick's Swan (Cygnus bewickii)

The Bewick's Swan is a smaller version of the Whooper Swan. We did not have any Bewick's Swans at Airlie, so my observations were limited to the few that I saw while in England. While it is believed that Trumpeter and Tundra Swans occasionally hybridize in the wild, I do not know if similar studies have been conducted on the Whooper and the Bewick's. With currently available DNA testing, much more can be gleaned about the differentiation of the species.

Black Swan (Cygnus atratus)

The Black Swan breeds mainly in Australia, although it is often kept by private owners and parks because of its grace and beauty. It has a melodic song, a protruding knob, a bright red bill with a white ring near its base, and white feathers on the underside of its black wings.

This is the swan that ignited my own passion. Although I had not yet seen it in person, I read about it and knew at that moment that I wanted to have swans in my life. During my time at Airlie, we had one Black Swan in the collection: John, whom I adored. Since the program was also host to several hybrids, he had become enamored with one of two Blutes, who were sisters. (The Blute is a cross between a Black Swan and a Mute Swan.) They had built a nest, but I never discovered if they actually laid any eggs. Both died a few years later, but Betty Blute remains as of this writing. She is a sweet but lonely swan.

Black–Necked Swan (Cygnus melancoryphus)

I will never forget the first time that I saw the Black–Necked Swan at the Denver Zoo, and later at the Richmond Zoo. Its song was beautiful and flute–like.

It is considerably smaller than our native species, boasting a bulbous red knob, a jet–black neck, and white body and feathers. Neither the Black Swan nor the Black–Necked Swan is migratory.

CHAPTER III

ESSENTIAL HABITAT

Perhaps at this point you have decided that you would like to have swans on your pond and you are also willing to accept the responsibilities and commitment that this requires.

I never like to consider myself the owner of any living animal, domestic or wild. Instead, I think of myself as the steward or the caretaker of those animals that share my living space, be they the migratory birds that are merely passing through, or the ones that, like my cats, share my life and even my bed. The bank may say that I own my property, but I know better. None of us can ever truly own even an inch of the earth, for as with any other of our possessions, we cannot take it with us when we leave here. At best, we can care for and nurture that which comes into the circle of our lives. I have always cared for the gardens wherever I have lived, be it my own property or one that I have rented. The Earth belongs to all of us, and it is our duty and responsibility to care for it and to protect it and all of its inhabitants while we are living here. I hope to leave this planet just a little better than I found it. This is why I care for everything that is placed in my care, be it animate or inanimate. I believe that we should treat other human beings, animals, and plants as we ourselves would like to be treated: with love and with respect.

The most important consideration in keeping swans is to ensure that you have proper habitat for them. If you are going to keep swans or other waterfowl, a pond is a necessary requirement. A pond of at least one acre in size is needed for a breeding pair of Trumpeters. You can probably get by with a smaller one if you are caring for other species or non-breeding birds. For the sake of cleanliness and sanitation, you should probably not house more than four or five birds per acre of pond space. Overcrowding leads to fighting and disease. If you are trying to breed and do not allow sufficient territory and habitat, the birds will likely not nest or lay eggs.

In the collection that I cared for at Airlie, we had more than 30 birds on the largest reservoir. Two pairs that had reached sexual maturity and were in their fourth year still had not tried to nest because there was no suitable site available to them. The dominant pair, which had successfully bred for the past four years, would run off all the other birds from two connecting ponds which they alone used. Prior to this pair having nested, they had exhibited their newly acquired dominance by chasing off the original nesting pair from Dr. Sladen's original ultra-light experiment.

Another interesting observation was that the female of this pair was one of the offspring of the original pair. Perhaps she found some comfort in this nest site, as it was the one in which she herself had hatched. I witnessed this same phenomenon with another ultra-light pair when, after they had passed on, one of their female offspring chose the same nest site with her new partner. I would be curious to know how often this occurs in the wild.

The Pond

Your pond habitat must be carefully analyzed to ensure that it will provide the best possible conditions for the health and safety of your swans. It goes without saying that water quality is of utmost importance for any type of waterfowl, since they spend the majority of their time in the water and drink and feed from it. You must consider not only the pond itself, but also the riparian area immediately surrounding the pond, the extent of wetlands outside the pond, and the source of water that feeds your pond.

What is the approximate size of your pond? Actually, it is possible to find the exact size if you know how to use Google maps or other similar computerized aerial photography of your property. For swans, the larger the pond, the better, remembering that at least an acre is required for a pair of breeding Trumpeter Swans.

What is the minimum and maximum depth of your pond? This is important, because if your pond is too deep, the swans will not be able to reach down to pull up the food plants from the bottom. A pond with a gradual slope is best. The swans will feed along the pond edges at depths of 3' to 4'.

What is the extent of the wetlands outside your pond? During early spring, swans may be found foraging along stream banks and vernal pool areas to enjoy the fresh green plants that are just emerging. The wetland areas that exist around your pond will provide an abundance of natural food sources for your swan's diet.

Have you allowed a riparian buffer to grow up around your pond? It is important to leave an area of 10' to 15' unmowed around your pond. This is vital to the health of your pond, as it provides shade and prevents water from overheating, which can cause algae blooms. The plants growing within the buffer help to slow down the runoff going into your pond and also act as a filter to hinder fertilizer and herbicide toxins from entering your pond. In fact, it is important that you not use these chemicals anywhere near your pond. You may mow a couple of narrow pathways through the buffer so that the swans have ease of access into and out of the water. Beyond the buffer, you may mow as you wish, since the swans prefer a flattened area to loaf and rest. This is more similar to their natural habitat, because they like to be able to see in every direction, giving them a clear view of any approaching predators.

What is the source of the water flowing into your pond? Is it fed from nearby streams? Is it spring–fed? A spring–fed pond is preferable, as a stream–fed pond will become the depository for silt and storm water runoff being washed into it.

Are there any chemicals (fertilizers, herbicides, pesticides) used in, near, or around the pond? If you are considering keeping swans, these practices must be stopped. Remember that swans eat those plants that you may have been trying to kill. Keeping swans is a natural way to clean your pond of unwanted sub-emergent plants. The water flowing in from nearby streams may be contaminated. Your neighbors up the hill from you may be farmers who allow their cattle access to the streams, which will quickly foul the water. Or maybe there is a nearby golf course that uses enormous quantities of weed killers and fertilizers. All of these and more can end up in your pond, which is your swan's living room, bedroom, dining room, and bath! It is advisable to get a water test done prior to bringing the swans to their new home and addressing any problems that the test indicates that you may have.

Is there a raft or an island in your pond? An island with a

tree and other native vegetation is ideal for swan habitat. A tree will provide welcome shade to a mother who is incubating eggs. The island itself will provide the greatest security from the threat of predators if it is properly maintained. This means keeping it mowed and free of brambles or other vines on which the swans can trip or in which they can become entangled. It is especially important when families are being raised, as the cygnets can be easily caught. Taller plants and grasses also provide cover for predators, which may be hiding in wait to snatch an unsuspecting cygnet. An island is generally the preferred nesting site for a breeding pair, and it is the safest place for them to nest. Swans prefer to spend their nights on an island or raft or floating in open water.

If you do not have a naturally occurring island, you can build a raft of suitable size. Another option is to look into the floating islands that are made from recycled plastic. I purchased one of these for my pond, and Henrietta, my resident female swan, spent at least 70 percent of her time on it. It is kind of cushy, like a mattress, and probably felt to her like the natural grasses that she may have rested on in the wild. The floating islands are a bit pricey, but they are well worth the cost. Another great advantage of the floating island is that it is made to have plants growing on it, so that the roots extend underneath it into the water, cleansing it of impurities and providing cover for fish. They are also available in many sizes. More information for building a suitable raft in lieu of an existing island is provided in this chapter under "Islands and Rafts."

Does a portion of your pond remain ice–free in winter? This is imperative. If it is known to freeze, you will need to use a deicer of some type to maintain open water for your swans during the winter season. A year–round aerator is really your pond's best friend. If you can afford to put one in, your investment will pay for itself by providing a healthy habitat. If you use only the deicer in winter, it is recommended that you pull it out at the end of the season, then clean and store it. This also allows you to check it for any damage and repairs that may need to be done prior to reinstalling it the following autumn. If you leave the deicer in year round, you run the risk of having problems at a time when the pond may already be freezing up. Muskrats love to chew through the electric cords, so a little prevention and proper care of your investment will save you money down the road. You can find a list of suppliers in the resources page at the end of this book.

Is there electricity access to the pond for a working aerator or deicer? You will need to know if it is 110V or 220V or higher, as this will determine the size of aerator that you install. Aerators can be simple affairs that generate bubbles just at the surface, or they can be elaborate fountains. It comes down to preference and budget—and, of course, the size of the pond.

Are there other waterfowl in your pond? If so, are they wild, captive, or domestic? Signs of other wildlife in and around your pond can be an indication of a healthy pond. If you have herons, swallows, and red-winged blackbirds, it is obviously to their liking and probably supports a vast array of species such as frogs and turtles. Too many domestic geese or Canada geese, however, can overburden a pond and create competition for food sources. Make a note of the birds visiting your pond and also of the fish it harbors. Catfish stir up impurities that reduce the pond's cleanliness and affect the water purity.

Is your pond located within sight of your home or office building? It is important for you to be able to see and monitor the swans on a daily basis. An ideal situation is to have the pond situated so that it can be viewed from a window, such as in an office or kitchen. You will want to have a pair of binoculars nearby, so that any unusual or interesting behavior can be easily monitored. You may even want to set up a telescope for the best viewing. If it is within your budget, consider building a small blind, where wildlife and your swans can be viewed without disturbing them.

Is there a fence around your pond? This may be impractical with a very large pond. However, there are several reasons to consider erecting a fence. If your swans are pinioned or feather clipped, they may still wander by foot. This puts them at risk of predation, and if there is a busy road nearby, they can be run over. Chasing down a swan that has escaped, even a pinioned one, is stressful for the bird and challenging even if you are young and fit. A fence of 5' or 6' can keep most predators out, and if you are concerned about vandals, a fence provides added protection for your swans. Adding an additional 6" or 8" border of barbed wire on top of the existing fence will provide added protection.

Check the proximity of busy roads to your property and pond. Vehicles seldom slow down or stop for most animals attempting to cross the road, and a swan is no exception. A flying swan's biggest obstacle is power lines, but a bird that has been rendered flightless can face multiple dangers with which it has had no experience.

For your convenience, I am including a Pond Habitat Assessment chart later in this chapter. You can use it to determine if your pond is adequate for swans. If, after completing your assessment, you are sure that you want to proceed with taking on the rewarding commitment of swan stewardship, then you can set about making any necessary changes and providing the necessary islands and aerators.

Once you have your pond, it is a good idea to have the water tested to be sure there is nothing potentially harmful in it. You will need to inspect it for the presence of SAV (submerged aquatic vegetation), which will hopefully provide the bulk of your swan's diet. At Airlie, we had an abundance of *Potamageeton crispus* in the early spring, followed by *Hydrilla* and common duckweed as the season progressed. Duck potato, or *Sagittaria latifolia,* is also a favorite of waterfowl. Parents will often guide their cygnets to feed on these miniature plants floating on the pond surface when they are still too small to feed from the pond bottom. The parents will also wriggle their feet to agitate the water and bring plants up to the surface for their young. If your pond does not have these naturally occurring plants, you can often bring them from other ponds and they will readily take root. They are often brought in on the feet of visiting Canada geese. If you are using a public pond where these plants are routinely killed, you may want to reconsider using that pond as a home for swans. Not only will it not provide the food that the swans require for optimum health, but the chemicals used to kill the SAV are potentially harmful to the swans.

Ideally, you may be able to educate those who instigate these harmful practices and help them to see the importance of maintaining a chemical–free habitat. Ignorance of our natural world seems to run amok, but knowledge is like a holy grail. If we can help one person see the error of their ways and change the way that they do things, then we have made a difference.

You need to look around the edges of your pond for common native plants and grasses. Depending upon the time of year, you may find an abundance or a serious lack thereof. If the grass around the pond has been cut all the way down to the water's edge, this is a practice that you will want to cease. A riparian buffer of at least 10' around the perimeter of a pond is essential to its health. It will help to slow down runoff and reduce soil erosion. It also helps in preventing fertilizers, herbicides, and pesticides from reaching and contaminating the water and fostering algae blooms in your pond. Perhaps there is a low-lying area or vernal pool nearby. Or you may want to consider adding a rain garden to help protect the quality of your water.

Riparian Buffers and Wetlands

Water quality is one of your primary considerations when providing for any kind of waterfowl. In this chapter, under "Wetland Habitat Assessment," you will find a list of plants that you may find growing in or around your pond. I have listed mostly native plants, but a few others are included to help you in determining which ones are invasive, so that you may consider taking steps to eliminate those plants. Depending on where you live, the plants listed may or may not be found in your area, but the best practice is to always plant and encourage native plants. By having a large variety of native plants, which include native grasses, sedges, and reeds, you will attract the native wildlife and other native waterfowl that depend upon these plants for their food and cover. For more in-depth information, you should be able to obtain resources from the U.S. Fish and Wildlife Service, your local and state wildlife departments, local native plant societies, and environmental organizations.

You may begin to see interesting intra-species relationships. For example, I have often seen cormorants sharing an island with a nesting Canada goose. Toward late summer and early fall, I would see the graceful white egrets fishing right next to the swans. The more friendly and hospitable that you make your pond, the more birds you will see stopping by to visit.

To create and maintain healthy habitat, it is imperative that you allow a riparian buffer to grow up around the pond, at least 10' or 15' out from the water's edge. If you have a very large property with streams feeding your pond and wetlands surrounding it, the riparian buffer should extend for 25' to 100' from the stream sides. The riparian buffer is a strip of vegetation that will improve and maintain the quality of your water by providing shade, which cuts down on algae growth.

When you mow too close to the water's edge, the grass clippings enter the water by way of wind and rain; once in the water, the clippings begin to decompose and create ammonia, depriving the water of oxygen. In addition, runoff from rainwater often contains excessive nutrient fertilizers, such as nitrogen and phosphorous. These chemicals may have entered the water from miles and miles above your pond, from farms, golf courses, and homeowners' lawns. Added to the chemical fertilizers are any number of toxic herbicides and pesticides, which result in a chemical soup. The result of this potpourri of dangerous chemicals, combined with sunlight, warm temperatures, shallow water, and stagnancy, is a foul–smelling algae bloom that ultimately becomes lethal to the aquatic organisms—which, under normal circumstances, keep your pond in a healthy balance. When your pond is deprived of needed oxygen, you will also have dead fish, which exacerbates the foul odor.

You will want to encourage native plants in the form of trees, shrubs, and flowering plants to grow in your buffer. This will also prevent soil erosion and sediment from entering the pond. The native grasses and shrubs will help to anchor your stream bank, thus providing stronger stabilization in the structure of your pond. The buffer also serves as a corridor for other wildlife whose habitat has been destroyed.

Pond Habitat Assessment

SITE CONSIDERATIONS	NOTES
What is the approximate size of the pond?	
What are the minimum and the maximum depths of the pond? Is the slope gradual, or does it drop off suddenly?	
What is the extent of wetlands outside the pond?	
Does the pond have a riparian buffer? If so, to what extent?	
What source is the pond fed from? How is the water quality?	
Are chemical fertilizers, herbicides or pesticides used in or nearby the pond?	
Is there an island or a raft in the pond? If yes, what size? Is there vegetation growing on it? What kind?	
Does any portion of the pond remain ice–free in winter?	
Is there electricity access to the pond for a working aerator? 110V or 220V?	
Are there other waterfowl in the pond? If so, wild/captive/domestic? What kind?	
Is the pond within sight of the house for monitoring swans?	
Is there a fence around the pond? If yes, what kind, how tall? Will it keep swans in? Predators out?	
Is the pond close to a road? If so, how close?	
Do dogs have access to the pond? If yes, what breed? How large? How many? Will they pose a threat to the swans?	
Is there SAV (submergent aquatic vegetation) growing in the pond? If yes, what type? (Take a sample.)	
Is the pond used for fishing? Have lead sinkers been used?	

Wetland Habitat Assessment

Here are charts for determining the wetland plants that you may or may not have. You will need to make a study of your habitat three times—during the spring, summer, and autumn—to determine if your habitat is adequate. You should ideally have at least 50 percent of these plants over these three seasons—depending, of course, on the bloom time or peak time of any particular plant. This list is by no means complete, and since it is based on plants found in the Piedmont area of Virginia, your own plants will vary depending on what part of the country you live in.

Note: In column three, N=Native, A=Alien, I=Invasive

Pond Trees and Shrubs

Pond Trees & Shrubs	Latin Name	N A I	1st Visit Spring Y—N	2nd Visit Summer Y—N	3rd Visit Autumn Y—N
Alder	Alnus serrulata	N			
Dogwood	Cornus florida	N			
Persimmon	Diospyros virginiana	N			
Willow, black	Salix nigra	N			
Willow, weeping	Salix babylonica	A			
Buttonbush	Cephalanthus occidentalis	N			
Elderberry	Sambucus canadensis	N			
Willow Oak	Quercus phellos	N			

Grasses

Grasses	Latin Name	NAI	1st Visit Spring Y—N	2nd Visit Summer Y—N	3rd Visit Autumn Y—N
Small carpetgrass	*Artrhaxon hispidus*	I			
Broomsedge	*Andropogon virginicus*	N			
Big Bluestem	*Andropogon gerardii*	N			
Little Bluestem	*Schizachyrium scoparium*	N			
Purpletop	*Tridens flavus*	N			

Submergent Aquatic Plants

Submergent Aquatic Plants	Latin Name	NAI	1st Visit Spring Y—N	2nd Visit Summer Y—N	3rd Visit Autumn Y—N
Curly–leaf Pondweed	*Potamogeton crispus*	I			
Hydrilla	*Hydrilla verticillata*	I			
American Pondweed	*Potamogeton nodosus*	N			
Arrow Arum	*Peltandra virginica*	N			
Water Arum	*Calla palustrus*	N			
Broadleaf Arrowhead	*Sagittaria latifolia*	N			
Arumleaf Arrowhead	*Sagittaria cuneata*	N			
Cattail	*Typha latifolia*	N			
Common Duckweed	*Lemna minor*	N			
Pickerelweed	*Pontederia cordata*	N			

Emergent and Flowering Plants

Emergent & Flowering Plants	Latin Name	N A I	1st Visit Spring Y—N	2nd Visit Summer Y—N	3rd Visit Au- tumn Y—N
Agrimony, Small Flowered	*Agrimonia parviflora*	N			
Aster , New England	*Symphyotrichum novae-angliae*	N			
Bur Marigold	*Bidens chrysanthemoides*	N			
Blackberry	*Rubus*	N			
Black-Eyed Susan	*Rudbeckia fulgida*	N			
Blazing-Star	*Chamaelirium luteum*	N			
Blue Flag Iris	*Iris versicolor*	N			
Blue Vervain	*Verbena hastata*	N			
Boneset	*Eupatorium perfoliatum*	N			
Butterflyweed	*Asclepias tuberosa*	N			
Bur-reed, American	*Sparganium americanum*	N			
Goldenrod, Canadian	*Solidago canadensis*	N			
Cardinal Flower	*Lobelia cardinalis*	N			
Great Blue Lobelia	*Lobelia syphilitica*	N			
Cattail	*Typha latifolia*	N			
Chicory	*Cichorium*	A			
Coneflower	*Rudbeckia laciniata*	N			
Fleabane, annual	*Erigeron annuus*	N			
Goldenrod	*Solidago rugosa*	N			
Ironweed	*Venronia novaboracensis*	N			
Jewelweed	*Impatiens capensis*	N			
Joe-Pye Weed	*Eutrochium purpureum*	N			
Knapweed	*Centaurea vochinensis*	I			
Marsh Marigold	*Caltha palustris*	N			
Milkweed, Common	*Asclepias syriaca*	N			
Mistflower	*Eupatorium*	N			

	coelestinum				
Monkey Flower	*Mimulus alatus*	N			
Pilewort	*Erechtites hieracifolia*	N			
Poke	*Phytolacca Americana*	N			
Queen Anne's Lace	*Duacus carota*	I			
Ragweed	*Ambrosia artimisiifolia*	N			
Smartweed	*Polygonum*	N			
Sneezeweed	*Helenium autumnale*	N			
Sow Thistle	*Sonchus arvensis*	N			
Spiderwort	*Tradescanti virginiana*	N			
Swamp Milkweed	*Asclepias incarnata*	N			
Swamp Loosestrife	*Decodon verticillatus*	N			
Swamp Candles	*Lysimachia terrestris*	N			
Thistle, field	*Cirsium discolor*	N			
Turtlehead	*Chelone glabra*	N			
Virgina Bluebell	*Martensia virginica*	N			
Vervain, white	*Verbena urticifolia*	N			

Islands and Rafts

As noted earlier, a raft, or preferably an island, is essential for the safety and wellbeing of your swans. If they have been rendered flightless, this is the only means by which they can escape predators. During the winter, you will also need to ensure that the area around the island remains ice free. Most predators will not try to cross open water; however, they will walk across ice that will sustain their weight. It is this area of open water between the swans and a would–be predator that provides the swans some assurance of safety.

A natural island is, of course, the first choice. It should be kept free of tall weeds and shrubs so that the swans have a clear view of any approaching danger. If your swans are breeding, it is also important to cut down any vines in which the cygnets can become tangled. Their webbed feet, being prone to injuries, will fare better on smoother, grassy surfaces. It is important to do any weed eating or maintenance of the pond well in advance of the nesting season, so that you do not disturb the swans once they begin building their nests. They will also appreciate extra straw that you may provide for them if enough natural nesting materials are not available. You can simply throw out a bale or a pile and they will place it in the manner that suits them. For a greater sense of safety, the swans will generally retire around dusk to an available island to sleep.

There are some newer man–made islands available, now, through some of the emerging environmental companies. They are offered in varying sizes and shapes, depending on the size of your pond. The one that I had was made of recycled plastic. It was covered with several small planting holes, which I planted with wetland plants in a medium of peat moss before launching the island into the pond and anchoring it. As the plants grew, the roots reached down through the plastic into the water below, where they provided cover for the fish and filtering capacity for toxins in the water. My female swan, Henrietta, loved her island, and I could understand why. It had a cushy feel to it, not unlike a mattress for a bed. Since she was older, I am sure that, like mine, her old bones appreciated the softness. A sloped side allowed for easy access to and from the water.

I was thrilled to look out one day and see Henrietta, Rose (my resident Canada goose), and a great blue heron all on the island at the same time. It was a small island of only about 25 sq. ft. Rose and her partner, Rambo, nested on the island for the two years that I was there. I am sure that this felt like a castle to them, since most geese are relegated to the edges of ponds. Sometimes geese lay their eggs too close to the edge or on too steep a slope, so that they roll off into the water. Consequently, each spring, I found a few eggs lying at the bottom of ponds.

If your pond does not have a natural island, and the floating island is not in your budget, you will need to resort to building a raft, which must then be anchored. The rafts that we typically used were made of two pieces of plywood with a float made of PVC pipe. A small slope was attached to one side of each raft to assist the swans in accessing and leaving them. See the illustrations below.

A small square was built into the center of the raft for the bird to build its nest. We would have to provide straw once or twice prior to nesting season, so that they would have nesting material. Because the swan program was a non-profit, the local farm co-op would let me have the waste straw from the bottom of their trucks for nothing, rather than my having to pay upwards of $6 per bale. I purchased paper lawn and leaf bags, which are much stronger than plastic (as well as better for the environment), and then I scooped up straw from their truck floors.

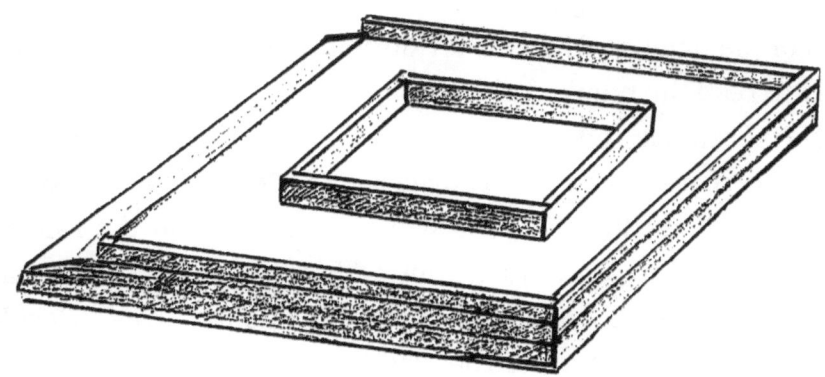

Handmade Wooden Platform

Manufactured Floating Island

I believe I can improve upon the basic raft which was made for use at the Swan Research Program. I would make an edge around the three unsloped sides and fill it with peat moss. I would plant it with clover and native wetland grasses and allow a few weeks for the plants to become established before anchoring the raft in the water. Not only would it look nicer, but it would also be more inviting to the geese and swans using it.

Anchoring the raft is a bit of a chore. You will first need to measure the depth of the water at the approximate place where you intend to set the raft. A tall bamboo stalk makes an excellent tool for this purpose. We conveniently had a grove of bamboo nearby. After cutting a very tall stalk, I would mark measurements along the side of the stalk. Then, submerging one end of the bamboo in the water until it hit the lake bottom, I was able to read the number of feet.

You can use rope to anchor the raft, but I recommend using powder-coated chain of ¼" or larger, depending on the size of raft you are anchoring. Rope will disintegrate and the raft will break free of its anchors within a short time. If muskrats are present, they will promptly chew through the rope. Regular chain will rust over time. The plastic-coated chain is a bit more expensive, but it will save you time and labor.

When measuring out your chain, count the number of links, so that all sides will be equal. We normally anchored only two corners, opposite each other. When measuring, be sure to account for what will be needed to go around the concrete block, or whatever you are using for an anchor. Also, account for the extra inches needed to attach the chain to the raft itself. To attach the chain, we screwed heavy-duty screw eye bolts into the sides of the raft. We then used stainless steel quick links to attach the chain to the raft and to the anchors.

Once you have your chain measured out and attached to the raft and to the anchors with quick links, you will need to place the anchors into the boat and row it, pulling the raft to the place you want it. It helps to have another person nearby on the shore to tell you when the placement looks good. Drop one of the anchors and then row out in the opposite direction until your chain is not quite taut before dropping the second anchor. This will allow the raft to move with the breeze, rather than creating tension that can cause the chain to break.

Be sure to have an ample number of rafts or islands. At least one raft for each breeding pair is best, depending upon the number of birds living in your pond. The moorings on the rafts should be monitored on a regular basis, and especially before the onset of cold weather, as anchoring rafts in icy cold water can be dangerous, not to mention not very fun.

Aerators and Deicers

The ideal pond habitat is one where there is constant movement, circulation, and aeration of the water. Without this, a pond can quickly become stagnant and overgrown with algae. The entire pond ecosystem will then suffer from poor health. Short of having a natural waterfall flowing into your pond, you may choose to use artificial means to maintain its habitability. There are varying types of aerators and fountains to suit both the size of your pond and your budget.

A simple aerator will merely stir up the water from just below the surface, where it can barely be seen. If you want to make an aesthetic statement, you can install one or more of the fountain–type aerators. Also, depending on the size of the motor, you will need to run 110 or 220 voltage down to your pond. The downside is that the aerators can be a bit noisy and do require some maintenance.

If your pond freezes up in the winter and you do not wish to maintain an aerator year round, you will still need to put in a deicer during the winter months. It is recommended that the deicer be removed, cleaned, and stored during warmer months, especially if you have muskrats, who love to chew through the electrical cords. The one that we typically used at Airlie was the Ice–Away, purchased from the Air–O–Lator Corporation. These are available with either a 50' or a 100' power cord. You may also want to check out aerators offered by The Pond Guy and by Otterbine Barebo, Inc. Please refer to the sources that are listed at the end of the book.

The deicer will need to be attached to a float. A simple float can be made using 3" or 4" PVC pipe. Have the pipe cut into four equal lengths. Attach corner pieces with PVC cement to create a square and seal with silicone around the outside seams.

Again, you will need to measure the depth of the water at the site of installation. Chain is stronger and less likely to break than rope. I prefer the powder–coated chain, which resists rusting. You will also need to measure how deep you want the deicer underneath the water. The closer to the surface that the deicer sits, the more bubbling effect you will achieve. Measure accurately to ensure proper placement. The two chains that you attach to the motor will be shorter than the ones used for the anchors. As with the rafts, attach the chain around two opposite corners of the float and attach the opposite ends to a weight, such as a cinder block. Then attach the other two chains to the deicer itself.

When you have assembled your float and attached your weights and your deicer, you are ready to put it in the boat and row it out to your drop location. You must consider carefully where best to place your deicer. It should be placed adjacent to a raft or island to ensure that there is open water around it. It is best to place the feeder in line with the open water as well. If you are using the Ice–Away deicer, it will have either a 50' cord or a 100' cord, depending on how close to your electric supply it will be situated. Be sure to attach the plug to the post where it will be plugged in before you head out into the water. This ensures that you do not drop the deicer too far away and that you will be able to plug it in. Do not plug it in until it has already been set in the water!

The deicers should always be in water whenever they are plugged in, or you can damage them. If you need to test one to make certain that it is working, you can attach it to a hook from the ceiling of a garage or carport and lower it into a barrel of water. Be prepared to get wet if the motor is working properly!

When you have rowed out to your drop location, drop one anchor and then row out until the other chain is not quite taut. Then drop that one. Carefully lower the deicer, with chains attached, into the center of the float. It is important that the deicer hang evenly from the chains, so it is imperative that your chains be exactly the same length. The best way to ensure this is to count the links on the chain.

One final note: Install your deicer early enough in the fall, before the pond has a chance to freeze. We once waited too long and had to break ice just to get the boat out to where we needed it. Putting your fingers into ice–cold water to attach chain is best avoided!

Feeding and Feeders

Swans normally feed on submerged aquatic vegetation— that is, plants that grow underwater. For this reason, the feeders should be placed out where the water is about 3' deep. The ideal depth for the swans to be able to reach the underwater food is around 3' to 4'. Swans that are feeding on the underwater vegetation stretch their necks down into the water to pull up plants from the roots. This is referred to as "upending," or "bottoms-up." This is why you will often see only the swan's bottom appearing above the surface of the water, with its large webbed feet helping it to balance. Supplemental feeding is essential for captive swans that do not have the ability to seek out their own food sources when their pond is no longer providing for their nutritive needs. We typically provided whole corn, which was really inferior nutritionally, but the non-profit status of the organization that I worked for prevented us from spending more than absolutely necessary. Because corn is basically junk food, I often wondered if feeding it to the swans was causing more harm than good.

There are pros and cons to the feeders that were used at the Swan Research Program. I will describe them in detail along with some of the disadvantages.

We used galvanized steel dog food feeders, generally the 50 lb. holding capacity ones, to accommodate a 50 lb. bag of corn. To the back of the feeder, we attached a thin block of wood, about as long and as wide as the back of the feeder. Two 1" C-clamps were placed in the center, one above the other and approximately 4" to 5" apart. Holes were drilled at each end of the C-clamps, all the way through the wood and through the metal feeder itself. The C-clamps were then attached with a washer and a flat-end screw, long enough to accommodate the thickness. Accuracy in measuring is crucial, because these C-clamps will then need to slide over a 1" thick rebar. We used the same 7' rebar for the feeders that we used for the setup of pens and traps. The rebar is pounded in with a post pounder to a depth of approximately 1.5'. Slide a hose clamp over the rebar and tighten just enough to keep it from slipping down. Place the bottom C-clamp (which is now attached to the feeder) over the rebar. Then place another hose clamp and then the top C–clamp over the rebar.

Measure the distance from the surface of the water to the bottom of the feeder, adjusting the hose clamps so that the bottom of the feeder sits about 30" above the water's surface. It is recommended that you have the feeder between 27" and 31" from the surface of the water. I was always admonished to keep the feeders high enough to prevent the Canada geese from getting the corn that was meant for the swans. However, I found that the smaller swans, such as the Tundra Swans and a few of the hybrids, had a difficult time reaching the 30" height. If you have smaller swans (Tundra) and larger swans (Trumpeters) and more than one feeder, you can place them at varying heights between those parameters. This will make it easier for the smaller swans to reach into them.

Be sure to tighten both of the hose clamps enough to prevent slippage. I cannot stress this enough. On several occasions, after I had added 50 lbs. of corn to the feeder, the entire thing slipped into the water because I had not tightened the hose clamps sufficiently. In my experience, only one hose clamp was ever used (beneath the bottom C–clamp). In retrospect, I believe that a second hose clamp placed beneath the top C–clamp would have prevented this problem. Also, I believe that having the second hose clamp would prevent the feeder from leaning to one side or the other, as they were prone to do. As the swans continually stretched and reached into the feeder, they would inevitably pull it forward, so after a time, they usually managed to pull the entire thing into the water.

You will save yourself a great deal of time and frustration by ensuring that your rebar is pounded in securely, because heavy rains can bring a feeder down, especially when the rebar has not been pounded in deeply enough, or when the pond surface is too mushy. A great deal of my time was spent re-setting and re-locating feeders.

I was always frustrated with the above-described feeder and wanted to come up with a more suitable alternative, but the nonprofit status of the organization put a crimp in my ability to seek out other feeders.

Dr. Sladen preferred to hang a smaller, 10-15 lb. feeder on a chain from a pier; however, this too requires diligent monitoring of the distance from the bottom of the feeder to the water's surface. The feeders that we used would rust over time, and often the bottom lip of the feeder would tear. I worried that the swans would cut themselves on the sharp metal.

It also became necessary to poke or drill several holes in the bottom of the feeders for drainage, as the corn would quickly begin to spoil if it remained wet after a rain. When adding Start & Grow or Layena to it, it would quickly turn into a wet mush. If the food in the feeder is frequently getting wet from rain, you should consider placing it so that it is turned away from the prevailing winds.

If the water around your feeders freezes up frequently, consider relocating them so that they receive direct sunlight during this time of year.

Another type of feeder that I have seen used with some success is either a galvanized steel or hard rubber garbage can with a circular hole cut into the side, just large enough for the swan to thrust its head through. This had to be securely anchored in place at the very edge of the water, and the lid had to be strongly secured to prevent raccoons from getting it off. This, of course, would need to be moved up or down on the shoreline to accommodate the rise and fall of water levels after a rain.

In considering the placement of any feeder, it is important that it be in an open area away from trees or shrubs, behind which predators may be lurking.

I was continually confronted with competition from other wildlife that helped themselves to the corn meant for the swans. I did not mind, but the nonprofit for which I worked did, because the corn was costly. Raccoons were expert at getting into the feeders. We used to attach bungee cords to prevent them from opening the lid to the feeder, until one day I saw a raccoon actually sitting inside the feeder, eating to its heart's content. I watched it get down when it was finished and swim the short distance to the shore. Deer, too, simply walk out into the water and help themselves, since the feeder is at the perfect height for them. One day, much to my surprise, I opened the top of a feeder to fill it and discovered a male wood duck caught in it. I carefully extracted it and immediately called the biologist, who then checked it for injuries. Fortunately, it was not seriously hurt, and I was able to release it.

Swans and other waterfowl are prone to water- and air-borne diseases, so it is imperative that feeders be maintained. They must be periodically sterilized with Tek–Trol. Any wet food that remains in the feeders can very quickly become moldy, so it must be disposed of. In between periodic cleanings, if the feeder is empty, it can simply be removed and swished out in the pond to remove any wet food. It is far better to under–fill the feeders and check them more often than to risk adding fresh food to spoiled food. This will ensure less waste, as well as prevent other species from consuming your swan's food.

Watching a swan die after being infected with aspergillosis is horrific and heartbreaking. This is why it is important to monitor your swans on a daily basis. A swan holding its mouth open is a sign of a sick bird. A bird that is dying of aspergillosis will emit a terrible gurgling noise from its throat.

I was filling feeders one day when I heard a strange noise. When I turned around, I discovered that one of the swans I had helped to raise was producing this horrible sound every time he opened his mouth. I quickly grabbed him and transported him to the vet, but his illness was misdiagnosed. I was sent home with tubes and antibiotics, but he was gone by the following day. When I took him for the necropsy, I was sickened by the sight of the fungus growing amok inside his lungs, heart, and other vital organs, and I hate to think of how long he had been suffering. I felt even worse the next day when I went out to check on his partner. She was still healthy, but I felt terrible for taking him from her and not allowing them to have closure.

Aspergillosis is an infection of the respiratory tract caused by a fungus which is normally present in the environment. A bird that is already in a depressed state of health becomes vulnerable when the mold becomes abundant due to increased damp, decaying material in the environment. The ingestion of moldy corn or grain is the primary means by which the birds become infected. The spores multiply in the lungs and spread to other parts of the body, ultimately leading to asphyxiation. Waterfowl and scavengers are prone to the disease, but captive birds are by far the most vulnerable. It is not contagious between birds, but overcrowding and unsanitary conditions coupled with young, stressed, and/or weakened birds provide the perfect environment for this mold to grow. No treatment has been found to cure a sick bird once it has contracted aspergillosis. This is why it is imperative that feeders and feed be kept clean and dry.

While I was caring for the overcrowded collection of swans at Airlie, I had a couple who were consistently aggressive, but it was because they were the underdogs and they were truly hungry. The larger, younger, and more dominant swans often monopolized the feeders. A few of the more timid swans learned to hang back and wait until those more domineering swans had left the area before approaching the feeders. Others had learned that I was the one they could count on to bring the food, so they would often see me and hear my truck long before I had changed into my waders and filled a bucket with corn. They would often run up the hill to greet me, or help themselves to the corn as I was pouring it. I only observed this behavior during those times when the SAV had ceased growing in the winter and/or when the feeders were completely empty. During those times when natural food sources were abundant and the feeders remained filled, those same swans paid no attention to my arrival.

Upended Swan and Feeders

Essential Tools and Materials for the Swan Owner

Following is a list of items that you will want to have on hand:

- Extra-large kennel and blanket to cover
- Small metal bowl and bottled water for transporting
- Straw or shredded paper for bottom of kennel
- Rain boots or wellies
- Waders
- Buckets, cookie sheets, and scoops
- Bag of whole corn, cracked corn, or duck feed
- Boat, paddles, and paddle locks
- Small broom
- Emergency first aid for self and swans
- Rescue Remedy
- Swan wrap and self-sticking VELCRO®
- Scale (optional)
- Post pounder
- Tool box
- Long-cut aviation snips and bolt cutter
- Plenty of rope and bungee cords
- Plastic zip ties in various sizes
- 1" galvanized hose clamps (pipe strap)
- ¼" stainless steel quick links
- ¼" powder-coated chain
- 3" or larger screw eye bolts
- Binoculars and spotting scope
- Camera
- Journal and pencils (Rite in the Rain®)

Prior to undertaking the guardianship of swans, there are a few items that you may want to be certain you have. You will want to have a kennel available at all times in case there is an emergency and you need to transport a swan. An extra–large dog kennel is required for a Trumpeter to accommodate their size. If you are transporting a Tundra Swan or cygnets, a large one should suffice. If you do not have space to keep one assembled, it is possible to assemble them fairly quickly by using plastic zip ties instead of the clamps that are provided with the kennel. It is best to keep an assortment of zip ties in various sizes, since they will also be used in assembling traps. Keep a supply of straw or shredded paper available as well, since the bottom of the kennel needs to be cushioned to protect the swan's vulnerable webbed feet and ankles.

If you have accustomed your swan to eating corn, it is best to keep a bucket and scoop and a supply of fresh corn with you, in the event that you need to capture it. I have found the plastic scoops to be preferable to the metal ones simply because they are lighter weight, which makes it easier to scatter the corn. If you are attempting to trap a swan, you may also want to have a large stainless steel cookie sheet on which to offer the corn in lieu of tossing it into the water. Place the cookie sheet as close to the water's edge as possible, because the swans can easily choke otherwise. Offering them corn is like offering a bone to a dog. If they have learned to like it, they will generally approach you to get their treat.

Other items that you will want to have if you need to transport a swan are Rescue Remedy, a blanket, bottled water, and a small metal bowl.

Rescue Remedy is a combination of flower essences developed by Dr. Edward Bach in the early 1900s. It is a concentrated liquid created from wild flowers for the purpose of balancing negative emotions. It has proven to be highly effective with animals and is frequently used by wildlife rehabilitators.

The calming benefits of the flower essences are a godsend.

Draping a blanket over the kennel will darken the kennel interior and help to calm the bird. If you need to go very far or if the bird is already heat-stressed, you will want to provide water. You can offer water in the bowl along with lettuce or SAV, shallowly filled inside the kennel, or simply squirt the water from a sipper-type bottle into the sides of the bird's bill.

You will of course want to have rubber boots or wellies. You will probably be spending a great deal of time in and around the water and traipsing through mud. Whatever type boots you choose to wear, they should be easy to slip on and off for changing into and out of your waders. One of the most important and indispensable items is a good pair of waders. I actually had two pairs to accommodate the summer and winter temperature extremes. I used a pair made of lightweight Gor-Tex® in the summer and heavier-duty Neoprene in the winter. It is a real plus if you can find waders with a pocket or pouch for storing tools, small hardware, or trash.

I also recommend that you get the *bootfoot* waders. I tried the *stockingfoot* waders, which proved disastrous when I had to set up traps or retrieve swans from them. It is necessary to wear another type of shoe over the stockingfoot waders, and I found that quite often, I was trying to maneuver in thick mud. The mud would suck my feet down and pull the shoes right off. In most cases, I was not able to find the shoes once they had been swallowed up by the mud. Since I had to change into and out of waders several times a day, I found the bootfoot waders to be far more convenient. A good pair of waders is a bit pricey, but it is well worth the cost if you need to spend a lot of time getting in and out of the water. You must make sure that anyone who is assisting you with trapping also has a pair of waders.

It probably goes without saying that you will need to have a reliable boat and a good pair of paddles. A rowboat is preferable because you can carry needed items with you, but a kayak is easier to maneuver, so it really depends on what the particular circumstances require. If you are merely rowing out to an island to do nest checks, a rowboat is perfect. If you are trying to guide swans into a trap, a kayak might be your best bet. I had to make do with less than ideal equipment, and I often had only one dilapidated paddle to work with. It is advisable to wear a life jacket, especially if you are heading out alone, although I never had one available. Fortunately, I never encountered a life–threatening situation.

A small broom makes the best deterrent to an aggressive swan, since it will not hurt it. Swans have extremely powerful wings, and if you encounter an aggressive one, it can easily break your arm if you do not have protection.

This would be a good time to interject a strategy for dealing with an aggressive swan. In most cases, the swans will not be aggressive other than during the mating season. A hungry swan may also be aggressive at times. The best way to handle an aggressive swan is to stand your ground with your arms held out. This will allow you to look bigger than the swan and let it know that you are the dominant one in the situation.

A first aid kit for yourself is a good idea if you will be handling the swans, since occasionally a swan's toenail can get caught in your skin, among other minor injuries.

It is advisable to have an emergency kit for the swans, which should include Rescue Remedy, gauze, alcohol, Blood Stop, and antibiotic.

A swan wrap is worth its weight in gold whenever you need to handle a bird. I have included directions for making one in the chapter on trapping.

Also, an 8–12" strip of self–sticking VELCRO® for binding the feet is very important anytime that you need to immobilize a bird.

Although not essential, a scale of some type is helpful for weighing birds when caught, especially when you are concerned about their health. My personal preference is a baby scale as opposed to the free–hanging type.

A good, heavy–duty post pounder is essential for pounding in rebar that you will use for erecting feeders, pens, and traps. It is also wise to carry, or have available, a tool box with screwdrivers, pliers, scissors, and other practical tools, such as long–cut aviation snips for removing neck and tarsus bands. Large, heavy bolt cutters will be needed to cut chain that you use for anchoring rafts and deicers. An ample supply of rope, bungee cords, and plastic zip ties are required for building pens and traps. Have on hand plenty of hose clamps, screw eye bolts, and quick link chain connectors, as well.

Finally, you will want to have a good pair of binoculars with you at all times, as well as a good camera for documenting illness or injuries. A good spotting scope and a tripod are very helpful, but not essential. Be sure to have a journal and plenty of pens and pencils for recording important observations.

CHAPTER IV

SAFETY

A swan's webbed feet are designed for walking on the thick grasses of the tundra or the grassy areas surrounding a pond, not on paved roads, rocks, or gravel paths. Since a large number of swans today are kept in unnatural settings, the risk of injury is high.

Bumblefoot is a common condition seen in birds that try to maneuver over uneven terrain. These are large calluses or protrusions that usually appear on the bottom and sometimes the top of the foot. Somewhat similar to an abscess, an injury to the foot begins to fill with pus due to the loss of protective scales and from bacteria entering the wound. These lesions are probably painful and can cause crippling when left untreated. Normally, they are drained and treated with antibiotics by a qualified veterinarian. Prevention is the key here. Untreated, these lesions can lead to complete crippling and loss of the use of the foot, or in some cases, both feet. Needless to say, a crippled bird is forced to spend all of its time in the water or become vulnerable to predation. Swan habitats should mimic what the swans would normally encounter in the wild to minimize the possibility of foot injuries.

Overcrowding in non–native habitats is the biggest cause of diseases seen in waterfowl. They may be able to survive imperfect conditions, just as some Holocaust survivors survived imprisonment, but swans should be allowed to *thrive* and *flourish*, not merely survive. This is why you must be able to insure that you can provide the best possible living conditions before you purchase or adopt swans.

The accumulation of trash in the swans' environment is also a common yet preventable problem. I strongly recommend that you prohibit fishing in any pond where waterfowl are kept. Needless to say, the fishing line and the hooks can be the cause of painful injuries and death to the unsuspecting birds.

While I was still working as a volunteer, a call came in from a frantic owner whose Black Swan's tongue was hanging out. A team of four, which included me, loaded up boats and nets to capture the swan. Since the Black Swan was a male, he often fought with the male Mute Swan on the very small pond that was shared with at least five other swans and numerous ducks. The owner believed that the injury was the result of fighting, but after the veterinarian examined the swan, it was revealed that a long cut ran vertically on the underside of the swan's bill. The tongue was pushed back into its mouth and the cut sewn up. We kept the swan on our nursery pond in a predator–proof pen and I looked after it until it was healed. A few weeks later, we returned the swan to the owners, admonishing them to clean up their pond area, which was strewn with broken and rusty fencing, metal, and other debris. Most certainly the swan had sustained its injury on a piece of the trash that was lying around the pond.

I was appalled when a few months later we received another

call from the same owner. The swan's tongue was again protruding from beneath its bill. This time they told us to keep the bird. They did not want it back. Worst of all, the pond had remained in the same hazardous condition that we had found it in the first time, and they had made no effort to tidy it up. I am certain that at this point the cost of paying for the swan's capture, transport, and medical bills outweighed its value to the owners.

Once again, the swan was nursed back to health, and we later moved him to the larger reservoir with our other swans. Not long after that, I saw that his tongue was protruding through the hole in his bill yet again. He was having great difficulty eating and drinking. We found him dead on the ice a few days later.

The neglect of animals and birds in our care has become a serious problem in our modern world. Please, if you do not have the time or the willingness to properly provide for them, do not take them on to begin with! Good stewardship requires doing what is best for the animal or bird, not what will impress our friends or fatten our wallets.

Predators

Because a large majority of pond owners also have dogs, I need to emphasize the importance of keeping away any dogs that may represent a threat to your swans.

Swans consider any dog to be a predator, regardless of how friendly or gentle the dog may be. They will become stressed by the sight of a dog, so it is best that you keep dogs away from the swans as much as possible.

It may be impractical to put a fence around your entire pond if it is very large, but it will help to discourage many predators if you have one. If you do put up a fence, you will also need to keep vines and shrubs from growing up next to it, or raccoons, bears, and other wildlife will simply climb over it. Other animals may try to dig underneath the fence, so it is important to check the bottom of the fence frequently.

Again, the safest place for a swan is on an island or raft out in the middle of open water. I had a 5' chain link fence topped by about 6" of barbed wire around my pond. This merely deterred predators; it would not stop an animal determined to get inside. In truth, there is no absolutely foolproof means by which to discourage all predators, but if you are diligent and take precautions, your swans have a good chance of remaining safe and sound.

Although it is not always practical, it is advisable to have your pond fenced if you have a swan that likes to move about. During the mating season, most swans will be on the move. This is an especially vulnerable time. I have seen swans kill each other in disputes over territory, and this behavior is further exacerbated by shrinking available habitat.

Transporting

Unless you are fortunate enough to have wild swans fly into your pond uninvited, you will most likely retrieve the swans yourself or have them transported to you.

Swans and waterfowl are prone to foot injuries. Place several inches of straw or shredded paper on the bottom of the kennel before putting your swan in it. This will help to protect the swan's vulnerable feet from injury, as well as make it more comfortable.

Be sure to use a kennel that is of ample size. Extra–large

kennels are generally required. It probably goes without saying, but the kennel should be made of plastic, *not metal*, and with small air holes that will not be large enough for the swan to put its bill into. I learned this the hard way as one swan that I was transporting arrived at the destination with blood and scrapes around its bill.

If your swan will be in the carrier for a prolonged period of time, you will want to ensure that it is as comfortable as possible. Most of us have known the agony of being cramped into a small vehicle or seated in an airplane where we were unable to stretch out our legs or raise our head. Your swan will already be distressed from being removed from its natural environment, so you should at least provide ample space for it during what is a terrifying experience. It will be frightened and may be suffering, as well, if it is sick or has been injured in some way. A domesticated animal such as a dog or cat may be easily acclimated to car travel, but a swan is a wild animal, a fact that we must respect.

Swans can also succumb to broken legs, broken toes, and broken wings. We should take as many precautions as possible to prevent unnecessary suffering and the expense involved should we require veterinary care for them.

Always drape a blanket over the kennel when transporting swans, as in most cases this will help to keep them calm. Some swans will not tolerate any human intrusion and will want to throw themselves against the sides of the kennel or thrust their bills through the small holes of the kennel, seeking escape. I have seen them rip off their toenails and inflict abrasions on their bills and wings as they tried to free themselves. Toenails will often bleed profusely, and it can be very disconcerting to arrive at your destination, only to find your swan lying in a pool of blood.

Remember, transporting a swan is probably the biggest stressor that it will have to endure. The noise of traffic, the foreign smells, and the unfamiliar sights, added to the frustrating confinement, will take a toll on your swan's health and well-being. When you must transport a swan, always do so in the quickest, quietest, and gentlest way possible.

Administer Rescue Remedy before traveling with them. Ensure that they have water, and that the temperature is controlled as much as possible. Traveling in an enclosed van is preferable to an open pickup, so that you can use air conditioning to prevent their overheating and cut down on the noise and smells assaulting them.

At Swan Sanctuary, I had no choice but to transport swans in the back of my pickup, since it was the only vehicle I had available. I also had to use it to carry panels for the pens and traps, rebar, corn, and other materials. Situations are rarely ideal, but armed with knowledge, we can make the best choices in any given situation.

One final important note is to be sure to clean out and sterilize the kennel immediately after use, so that it will be ready the next time that it is needed. We used a strong germicide called Tek–Trol, but I imagine that chlorine bleach would suffice. Be sure to rinse the kennel thoroughly.

Lead Poisoning, Power Lines, and Other Dangers

Another serious consideration when assessing your pond is to find out whether or not it contains lead from fishing sinkers or from shot, if hunting has been allowed around the pond. It may be impossible to really know, or to remove any lead that might be lurking in the bottom of the pond, but you should at least familiarize yourself with the signs of lead poisoning in birds so you can take steps immediately to help any birds that have unwittingly ingested this most harmful material. Some of the symptoms of lead poisoning are not unlike the symptoms of aspergillosis, which include overall weakness, a rattling sound from the throat, a change in voice, and maintaining the bill in an open position.

During necropsy, a lead-poisoned bird will generally have an accumulation of lead in the gizzard, leading to its overall decay. The lead quickly moves to the muscles, where residue is retained in the wings and feet, creating paralysis. A wild bird will lose its ability to fly, making it easy to capture. While in the water, its primary feathers will dangle on the surface of the water, and if on land, it will lose its ability to walk. More than likely, the bird will also be suffering from anemia. Wild, lead-poisoned birds tend to lose 50 percent or more of their body weight, although captive birds do not necessarily show this symptom. You may also notice a yellow substance dribbling from the bird's bill, and vent staining caused by greenish, runny feces. Obviously, any unusual symptoms in your swans should be noted, and a seriously ill bird should be examined by a qualified avian veterinarian. If caught early, lead poisoning can be treated with some success.

If you have property and a pond of sufficient size (preferably an acre or more), you may want to consider providing a home for an older or incapacitated swan. This is the reason that I began Swan Sanctuary. From time to time, injured or sick swans are found and are in need of a safe environment to convalesce and live out their lives. Lead poisoning is a common cause of illness. Lead shot from hunters and lead sinkers from fisherman sink to the bottom of ponds and are subsequently ingested by the swans. In many cases, the lead may have been in the area for decades.

Whatcom County in Washington State, which sees a large number of Trumpeter Swans in winter due to the extensive wetlands, is also the site of many swan deaths. Fortunately, efforts are being made to clean up the lead, but there are still no federal bans in place to prohibit the use of this deadly substance.

Flying into power lines is common, too; that and lead poisoning are the largest threats to swans. Collisions almost always result in instant death by electrocution. This is a horrific and painful death.

The Avian Power Line Intervention Committee was established in the 1980s to address this issue, not only for swans, but also for whooping cranes and many of our larger migrating birds. Various devices and designs have been implemented in some areas to reduce collisions. Aerial marking spheres, spiral vibration clamps, and swan flight diverters are just a few of these remedies.

If you are concerned about this issue for your own birds, you should contact your electrical company to ascertain what solutions they can provide.

During my many years of caring for the swan collection at Airlie, Virginia, we lost at least three swans that were run over by automobiles. This never would have happened had the swans been allowed to fly.

Other threats to swans are illegal hunting, destruction of suitable nest sites, loss of habitat (especially wetland habitat), and loss of agricultural land, which provides food in winter when ponds are frozen over. New diseases are cropping up, as well, such as the avian influenza.

If you have a pond and proper habitat, you can provide a

much—needed service for swans who have become victims of the ever—increasing dangers that pose threats to their survival.

Emergencies

If you have taken on the serious commitment of swan stewardship, at some point you will inevitably need a reliable avian veterinarian and an emergency backup plan. If you plan to have swans and care for them, it is imperative that you acquire beforehand a reliable veterinarian who is experienced in treating avian species.

Avian specialist veterinarians are few and far between, but I cannot stress enough the importance of this. A vet who primarily works on dogs, cats, or horses is not always helpful, regardless of his or her good intentions.

You may also want to confirm that the vet will be available in emergency situations. Generally, when a swan is sick or injured, it *is* an emergency, so if the staff is ignorant, they may simply tell you that you will need to make an appointment. Find out ahead of time what you should do if, on the day that you require the veterinarian's services, he or she is out, because swans rarely adhere to an 8 to 5 schedule.

In addition, you must have an emergency protocol set up in advance, so that, should an emergency arise, you already have a plan in place. This plan should include the name and phone number of the veterinarian and a detailed map to the clinic, although a veterinarian who makes house calls is preferable. Transporting a wild bird, even a captive wild bird, increases its stress immensely, and this can be further increased if you are driving a long distance or in heavy traffic.

During transportation, always drape the kennel with a blanket, as the darkness will help to calm the swan. If at all possible, administer Rescue Remedy, as it has a proven calming effect. I always keep some with me for unexpected emergencies. If you can open the swan's bill slightly, use the dropper to deliver some directly, or simply rub some on the feathers close to the bill. If that is not possible, add it to water or food that you are providing.

You should have an extra-large dog kennel nearby that is always set up and ready, with straw to line the bottom. If you do not have straw, then blankets, shredded paper, or anything else that will cushion the kennel floor will suffice. Waterfowl frequently succumb to foot injuries, and the injuries often occur during transportation, so it is very important that the birds be moved in the kennel with extreme care, so as not to cause them to lose their balance.

I first became aware of the importance of having an emergency plan in place when I was still a volunteer and I was called to respond to an emergency. The Swan Research Program instituted an adoption program; we adopted out Mute Swans singly or in same-sex pairs to save them from euthanasia. One day I received a call from a very distraught man who had just pulled his swan from the water with a snapping turtle attached to its head! He had been unable to get hold of either of the biologists in charge, so I, being the only assistant available, drove the 25 miles to his property.

At the time his call came in, the swan was lying limp and bleeding in his daughter's arms, but when I arrived at his residence, the swan had escaped back into the water. We had to further stress the swan by running it down and capturing it. The adopters did not have a kennel, and neither did I. The veterinarian that I had recommended was more than two hours away. After a great deal of confusion and much arguing between the husband and wife, they finally agreed on which vet to take it to. The only two options were both over 40 miles away. I sat in the back of their station wagon holding the swan in my lap while it bled profusely.

Fortunately, when we finally arrived, the veterinarian was available, and she was somewhat experienced in treating birds. Unfortunately, the damage was very extensive and would have required further transporting to another veterinarian about 60 miles away, then back to her the following morning, followed by two or three months of rehabilitation and no guarantee that the swan would survive. I prayed that the owners would make the decision to put the poor swan out of its misery. Fortunately, they did.

In an emergency situation, even if a bird's life cannot be saved, it is our responsibility to take steps beforehand to be able to handle the emergency and to keep stress to a minimum. If for any reason you are unable to immediately transport a swan that you suspect is sick—for example, due to the time of day or the lack of availability of a veterinarian—you can place it in the kennel and place the kennel in a basement or garage where it is quiet. Cover the kennel with a blanket, and be sure to provide water and perhaps some lettuce.

Following is a list of things that you will want to have on hand for emergency situations:

- Extra–large dog kennel
- Plastic zip ties for quick assembly of the kennel, if it is not already assembled
- Straw or other material for lining the bottom of the kennel
- Blanket to cover the kennel
- Small shallow bowl for water
- Rescue Remedy to calm the bird
- Phone number, address, and map to the nearest avian veterinarian
- Waders, in case you have to retrieve the swan from the water
- Vehicle with full tank of gas
- First aid kit to control possible bleeding
- Camera for documenting scene and site of injury
- Blank data sheet or pencil and paper for recording time of day, swan identification, weight, and other pertinent information

CHAPTER V

BUILDING PENS AND TRAPS

If you plan on raising swans, as opposed to merely maintaining only one or two, you will at some point have need of a pen. An injured swan or one that has been recently pinioned will need to be confined for short periods of time. Also, if you plan to move a swan from one location to another, you may need to keep it in a holding pen for a few hours or longer.

At Swan Sanctuary, I had a dry pen and a wet pen.

A dry pen was sometimes needed if a swan had just been pinioned and needed to be kept out of the water for a few days, or in the case of an injury. A dry pen also served as an ideal place for raising orphaned cygnets or those that had been hatched in an incubator. A child's small wading pool could then be placed inside once the cygnets were big enough to be introduced to the water. Having a movable dry pen also lets you maintain cleanliness, so that the birds are not continually walking and eating in their own excrement, which can lead to disease.

Dry Pen

The dry pen can be set up anywhere, but preferably along the grassy edge of the pond. This will make transitioning from a dry to a wet pen much easier.

Since I rarely used the dry pen, I used a small fence–type dog kennel, which can be purchased at a farm or pet supply store, and which already has the gate on one side for entering and exiting. If a larger pen is required, kennels may be purchased in sizes of 5' or 6' in height by 8' or 10' in length. The advantage to purchasing the pre–made kennels is the inclusion of the gate. Sometimes these kennels come with optional roofs, but the important thing to remember is that the roofing material must be inaccessible to predators.

I attached only the sides of the pen to each other and did not anchor it in the ground. This allowed it to be moved every few days for mowing or weed eating, which was far easier than trying to mow or weed eat inside the pen. The down side is that it takes two or three people to move the pen and keep it intact, so this can be problematic if you are working alone.

A pen must be entirely predator–proof. Therefore it must have a top or roof of some type. A larger fence panel can be laid over the top of one of the small dog kennels with a tarp draped over it to provide shade. I have also used heavy–duty lattice over the top and secured the edges by weaving rope all the way around it. The roof must be made of a material that is strong enough that a raccoon or other predator cannot chew through it. I have used chicken wire, but it has sharp edges and can be difficult to work with.

You may also need to reinforce the bottom, so that animals cannot dig underneath it. Since the ground is rarely completely level, you may need to attach chicken wire around the outside bottom edges or place heavy cinder blocks or rocks around the edges.

As a final step, it is important to ensure that there is nothing on the *inside* of the pen that can injure the swan. The most suitable fabric to use as a cushion inside the pen that I have found is one that I purchased from an air conditioning supply firm. This fabric came in rolls that were 3' high by 30' long, so one roll provided enough fabric to cover three 10' fence panels. It was of a very thick, porous material, so that rain and water passed through it easily, and if the swans threw themselves against the sides of the pen, their wings were protected from injury, since they could not attain a leap much higher than 3'. The fabric also helped to cover any gaps and blocked predators from being able to see inside the pen. I used thin twine and a large yarn needle to sew the fabric to the inside of the panels. You can leave a few inches at the bottom and sew along that edge, too, as added insurance against predators.

Finally, the door on the pen must remain closed whenever there is no swan in it, because if a swan wanders in there on its own, a predator could follow it in and corner it. At nighttime, be sure to secure the door with plastic zip ties, bungee cords, or a padlock. At night, it is best to remove any food that might attract predators.

Wet Pen

Wet pens are more challenging to build because they are built at the water's edge, and you have to account for slope.

Pens can be made any size that you feel is necessary. Ours were constructed with 6' x 10' chain link panels and 1" rebar custom-cut to 7' lengths.

The slope and depth of your pond will determine how far out into the water you wish to build the pen. If it is for protecting a recently pinioned or injured bird, you will not want it in more than about 3' of water at the water's edge. This will allow the swan to drink and get its feet wet, but not fully submerge its body. If you simply want to keep swans separated from each other, you can build the pens farther out into the water.

Three chain link panels per side will make a pen of adequate size. If you can purchase one panel with a door already in it, this will make your life immensely easier. Otherwise, you will have to leave one side unattached for access, and this is challenging.

One of the biggest challenges in building a wet pen is working with the slope and with unforeseen rocks that present themselves at the exact spot where you are trying to sink your rebar. Rocks are difficult to see underwater, and there is no way of knowing how big they are. If the rebar is not going in after two or three tries with the post pounder, you will need to move it over a few inches until you find a suitable place. This is often difficult to do, and it can throw off the entire size and shape of the box you are trying to build.

Sometimes the mud is so thick that it will suck in the boots of your waders. This makes it difficult to maneuver, especially when you are carrying a heavy panel or rebar.

Add to that the weather conditions. I have worked in freezing cold temperatures when I could barely get my fingers to move, and also in sweltering heat, which was enhanced by the waders I was wearing. Some people just go right into the water in shorts, but that was not an option for me. I have built traps in clean, cool reservoirs and also in murky, swampy wetlands, but being around the swans and other waterfowl and birds was so joyful for me that I paid little attention to the conditions I was working in.

Begin building the sides of the pen first, working from the center outwards. This way, the ends can be tweaked in one direction or the other for size adjustment. Using a post pounder, place your first rebar near the edge of the pond. Attach one side of one panel to the rebar, using either 11" plastic zip ties or self-sticking VELCRO®. Pound in your second rebar the same distance out into the water as your panel is long (usually 10'). If you choose to add another panel out in the water, pound a second post the same distance out. Attach the panels to the rebar.

This is where it can get tricky. Depending on the slope of the terrain, at this point you will need to compensate for the difference in height. You will need to make certain that any gap left at the bottom is not large enough for the swan to swim underneath. It is best to have your gap at the top, which hopefully is no more than a few inches difference. Using cinder blocks to stabilize the panel that you are trying to attach is helpful if you do not have another person assisting you. Cinder blocks also make great stepping stools if you are short and have trouble reaching the top of the panels to attach ties or rope.

Note: When you are securing the fence panels to the rebar, it is very important that the center bar of the chain link panel be facing out. If the center bar is on the inside of the trap, the swans can easily injure themselves when they begin flapping about.

Once your side panels are attached, place your next panel between them, creating the third side of your pen. Once you have three sides in place that are encompassing water, complete the fourth side (which will be your door) on shore, making sure to leave the ends of the side panels unsecured until your corners are lined up.

If you are using plastic zip ties, *it is imperative that none accidentally fall into the water.* They could be ingested by the swans, causing suffering and possible death. Make sure that you are wearing waders with pockets or other suitable storage for these and for tools that you may need. Zip ties are efficient and quick, but I found that they are costly, and because they are not recyclable, I was contributing shamefully to already overloaded landfills.

Later, I began using self–sticking VELCRO®, which could be cut into suitable lengths and used over and over again. It was just as strong as the plastic, but it did not deteriorate and break apart and end up in the water, causing a hazardous situation for feeding swans.

The weathering and disintegration of plastic zip ties supports another argument that I have for not leaving pens or traps in place for extended periods of time. Zip ties become dry and brittle, snapping and breaking off. The chain link panels begin to rust and deteriorate when left too long in the water. Trap doors that are left up become warped, so they do not close properly.

It is far easier if you have a second person assisting you when building a pen or trap, but help was difficult to come by for me, and I figured out ways to manage to build them on my own.

Once you have three sides of your pen erected, if you want the pen to do double duty as a trap, you can attach a lighter–weight door where it will open into the water. In this case, refer to the following section on traps.

Now that you have three sides of your wet pen erected, you can place the entry door, which will be located on land.

If you do not have a panel with a pre–made door, you can use one of the handmade doors described on page 101, or simply use another chain link fence panel. The latter is the least desirable, because it is difficult to open and close, especially after you have attached roofing material. However, if you have no other choice, this will work. Just secure one side with zip ties or VELCRO® and use bungee cords on the side on which you wish to enter and exit.

The next step in securing your pen is to cover the entire top with something that is strong enough to keep out predators. The size of your pen may dictate what you use.

Anything made of plastic is not suitable, as raccoons can chew through it. Chicken wire is sharp and difficult to work with. If cost is not an issue, I think that 1" fencing cut to the size of your pen and attached securely all the way around with thin wire is the strongest. If you are using another fence panel for your door, however, you will need to leave it unattached just enough so that you have room to squeeze into the pen, holding a swan at the same time. This portion would then need to be secured with bungee cords.

The last step of creating your pen is to attach cushioning fabric completely around the inside and, most importantly, on the sides facing the water. It is the birds' instinct to head straight to the water to flee from danger, and often they will throw themselves violently against the door until they have completely worn themselves out. The fabric will soften their blows and reduce potential injuries. It also makes it more difficult for predators to see them.

Once it is erected, make a final inspection of your pen from top to bottom, looking for any holes that are large enough for a raccoon or snapping turtle or any other threat to find its way in. You want to make sure that what you have built is going to keep your swan safe and not become a death trap for it.

Lastly, it is important that you lay down a strip of sand along the water's edge. Swans have gizzards, and unlike us, they need grit to digest their food. You may provide sand in a dish along with a bucket of water in your dry pen.

Traps

If you are going to keep swans, it is more than likely that at some point you will need to catch them, either to move them to a new location or to feather clip or band them.

There are several types of traps. Quite often the type of trap that you use is determined by the terrain in and around the pond where you are working.

Traps are built pretty much the same way as the pens, but the challenging part is attaching the trap door (or doors) so that it (or they) will close quickly, smoothly, and flush; this last is very important. Traps may have one door or two doors, depending on how many swans you are catching and how accustomed they are to the trap. The size will also depend on how many birds you plan to trap. Traps may be built in the water, on land, or half in the water and half out. If you are making a trap on land, it is best to have it as near to the water as possible, close to a spot where the swans regularly walk into and out of the water.

At the Swan Research Program, we mostly used a simple affair of two sides with a trap door at each end.

Ideally, the trap is set up approximately two weeks before you actually plan to trap the birds. This allows the birds time to get used to its presence. The doors are left propped open in the beginning, in order to get the birds swimming (or walking) through it. The trap is baited several times a day by tossing just a small amount of corn into it. Baiting at the same time of day gets them used to visiting the trap at those times.

When you are ready to trap the birds, you can do so with the two–door method by having the trigger close both doors at once. This sometimes takes longer because you have to wait until the birds that you want to catch are at the center of the trap and that no birds are near the doors, where they may be struck by them on their way down.

Another option is to permanently close and secure one of the doors after the swans have grown somewhat used to the trap. This way you only have to worry about closing one door.

When using a one–door trap, be certain that the birds are at the end of the trap opposite the door before trying to close it. If they are too close to the door, they may escape before the door closes completely.

Another trap is the funnel trap, which is really just a variation on the straight trap. It can be curved and made narrower at the front end. Kayaks or boats can be used to funnel birds into this type of trap.

I have also heard of a rocket net trap being used, but with disastrous results. Dr. Sladen felt that they were dangerous and did not recommend using them, as they often result in the loss of birds' lives.

Most methods of capturing birds usually involve several people.

Kayaks can be used to steer them from the water to dry land, where other people are waiting to run them down. This is difficult because the birds are very fast when trying to make their escape, and it requires speed and skill on the part of those running after them. If you miss, you have really lost your window of opportunity, and it can take weeks to implement another plan that does not raise fear and suspicion in the birds. I do not recommend this method because I feel that it causes undue stress on the birds.

Sometimes you may be left with no other choice than to run a bird down if it has escaped your property or is injured or in danger of being injured, such as near a busy road.

We occasionally used large pole nets (used for fishing) to aid in capturing birds from a boat or even on land; however, I did not like using them. They were big and heavy and cumbersome, and once the bird was caught, it became extremely difficult to extract it from the net. In most cases, the netting holes were far too large, resulting in the swan's feet, bill, and feathers getting tangled in the net.

Birds that have been caught numerous times often become easier to catch as time goes on. Truly wild birds are far more difficult, as they are more suspicious and less trusting.

We would often sit in our vehicle with the windows down, right next to the trigger rope, because the swans were far less nervous when they could not see us. When that was not possible, we could hide behind a shrub or vehicle or other object so that the swans would not be aware of our presence. I also found that, because swans are territorial, it was often helpful to place a decoy in the trap when I was ready to trap swans.

Because swans will try to make their escape into the water, it is necessary to run as quickly as possible after you have triggered the door to close and then bungee the trap shut, beginning with the corner nearest to the water. If you have dropped the doors on a two-door trap, you will want to bungee the side that the swans are closest to first.

When building your traps, you will want to begin in the same way as when building a pen.

After determining the best location for your trap, erect the sides of your trap first. This will allow for the necessary tweaking when it comes to attaching the doors.

If you want your wet pen to double as a trap, in addition to the 7' rebar, you will also need a crossbar from which to hang the door. The crossbar needs to be at least 1' longer than the rebar, preferably 8' to 9' and of a lighter weight. The doors themselves also need to be constructed of a lighter–weight material than the galvanized fence panels. This is so that when the door is dropped, it will fall quickly and lightly; what is most important is that it fall flush with the sides of the trap. The doors also need to be slightly smaller in height than the fence panels and slightly wider than the distance between your two side panels, so that there will be no gap through which the swans can escape. If you are using 10' x 6' panels, the door size should be about 11' x 5.5'.

The doors used at the Swan Research Program were made of thin piping which had been soldered together to make the four sides and then had ¼" hardware cloth attached to it. The size of the hardware cloth, or whatever type fencing is used, is important because it needs to have smaller holes than the chain link panels. When trapped, the swans will head straight for the opening end of the enclosure to try to escape. If the holes are too large, they will thrust their bills and their feet through them, resulting in ripped toenails and abrasions to their bills. The problem that I found with the existing doors was that the hardware cloth had been attached with plastic zip ties, which had deteriorated and broken off. To remedy the problem, I made temporary repairs by weaving twine around the sides of the door and through the holes of the hardware cloth to reinforce it. This was *very* temporary, as the twine quickly weakened in the sunlight and water and began to break and unravel. It would be far better to use thin wire instead of twine, to ensure strength and to make them last longer. Since I was working for a non-profit, however, I often had to make do with what was on hand and find less expensive ways of doing things.

Also, since these doors and traps had been left up for months on end, they had become warped. This created many problems for me when trying to trap birds for feather clipping, as the doors would not close flush and the birds would escape before I could get the door secured.

Reattaching the fencing to the frame did nothing to address the warping problem, so I attempted to make new doors using ¾" PVC pipe and the plastic safety fencing that is commonly used at construction sites. I attached the fencing with twine, but it was not strong enough and broke loose in places. The door was also a bit too lightweight and did not close quickly enough. In retrospect, I would recommend using a slightly larger, heavier PVC pipe and attaching the plastic fencing with thin, plastic-coated wire, woven all the way around the edges.

I used 1" to 1.5" diameter hollow, galvanized steel piping for the crossbar for hanging the trap door. The length needs to be 4" to 6" wider than your opening to ensure that there is no gap at the corners when the door is closed. This bar can also be used to measure the distance between the side panels prior to attaching them to the rebar.

Accurate measuring is imperative, because if you secure the side panels and they end up being not quite parallel, the door panel may not reach to the other side, or it may overlap too far. It is important to attach the crossbar on the outside of the side panels in order for the door to close correctly.

Position your crossbar at the height at which, when the door is hung, the bottom will be even with the bottom of the trap. This may be below the water's edge. If there is too much distance between the lake bottom and the bottom of the door, the swan can swim underneath.

Use 6' rope lengths for all your connections, making sure that you have several pieces available. I found that all–purpose clothesline rope worked best. You must reinforce the ends of your cut pieces with waterproof tape to keep them from unraveling. Attach both ends of the crossbar to the ends of the pen sides using a sash–type knot. The crossbar should be attached to the outside ends of your side panels, using a combination of hangman and square knots to achieve a tight right angle between the bar and the panel to which you are attaching it.

You must also ensure that you place the bar high enough, and also low enough, so that once your door is hung from it, it will close swiftly and flush. You must make sure that there is not a gap between the bottom of the door and the pond bottom that is large enough for the swans to swim through. You may need to use a cinder block to stand on to reach the height at which you are placing your crossbar.

Once the crossbar is securely attached to the side panels, you will hang the door from the crossbar, attaching it in at least three places. You can use VELCRO® to hold it in place temporarily while you tie it securely with your precut ropes. You can also use a combination of rope and VELCRO®. If you are working alone, it helps to hold the door in place with bungee cords until you can get it secured.

Once the door is attached, hold it up and let it fall a couple of times to be sure that it is closing properly. Then, holding the door up (from the side closest to the shore), measure the distance straight out from the corner and pound in another rebar at that spot. Attach a small piece of wood, about 6" x 6", to the underside or inside of the bottom corner of the door. Plastic zip ties work best for this. This will allow the door to slide easily off the rebar when tripped. I always do a couple of test drives to make sure that the door is going to close as I have envisioned it will and to make any necessary adjustments.

You will want to leave the door propped up while the swans are becoming accustomed to it, so secure the door onto the rebar close to the piece of wood, but not directly on it. Double check to make sure that the door will not accidentally close when you are not there. A bird that is caught in the trap when you are not planning for it is vulnerable to injury and attack by predators.

If you plan to leave the door closed, you can secure the bottom corners with bungee cords. If you will keep it closed more permanently, you can secure it with zip ties or VELCRO®. The bungee cords will also deteriorate and break when left out in the weather for long periods of time, so I recommend not leaving them in place unless you plan on trapping birds within a short time span.

Once your door is attached (or both doors, if you are making a two-door trap), you will need to attach a 25' to 50' length of rope to the rebar that is holding up the door. Walk out to the place where you plan to hide and wait unseen, such as a hidden place behind a shrub, or where you can sit in your parked vehicle. Erect another rebar in this spot. Attach the other end of the rope to it, making sure that any excess length is bundled at the top, so that the swans or other animals are not at risk of becoming tangled in it.

Now that your trap is built, you will need to attach cushioning fabric to the insides to prevent the swans from injuring themselves once they are trapped inside. This would be the same fabric that you use in your pens: a porous, spongy material that can be purchased from an air conditioning supply firm. It should be attached so that the bottom of it just skims the surface of the water if your trap is in the water, or such that the bottom edge is even with the ground if your trap is on land.

If you do not have enough material to go around, it is most important to cushion the side that is closest to the water, as this is the direction in which the birds will go to try to make their escape. I cannot stress enough the importance of this. I witnessed many birds bleeding from injuries to their bills from trying to put them through the fence panels and injuries to their wings from throwing themselves against the fence. Quite often, their toes were bleeding as well, from toenails being caught and ripped off on the fencing. When trapping birds, it is imperative to do so in a manner that causes them the least amount of stress and to do so in as quick and efficient a manner as possible.

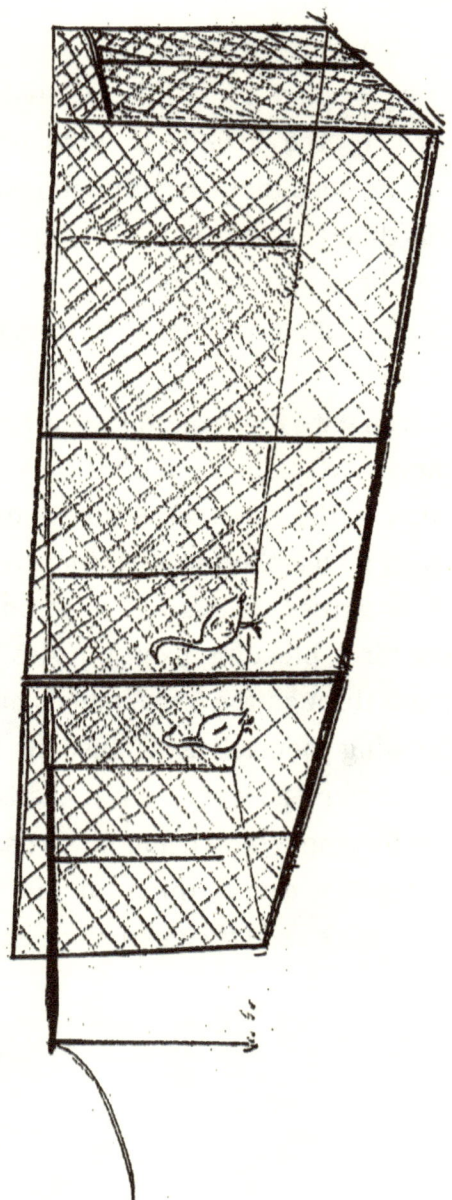

Trap Made of Chain Link Fence Panels

CHAPTER VI

TRAPPING

If you are only beginning to consider acquiring swans, you may wonder why I am including a section on traps and trapping.

I cannot emphasize enough that swans are wild animals and will not calmly acquiesce to your desire to keep them. In most circumstances, your swans will be delivered to you in a kennel after having been procured by someone else, but if you believe that all you must do after that point is enjoy watching them, then you have not been well informed. I have already addressed this issue in the first chapter, and I invite you to revisit the section *Why Keep Swans?* A bird that is seriously ill or injured may allow you to walk up to it without much resistance, but in most cases it will try to flee. For this reason, you must have a plan for capturing it, whether it is for a planned purpose or in case of an emergency.

Once your trap is installed and working properly, you will want to bait the trap at least twice a day. It is best to do this at the same time each day.

You can have your feeders near the trap, but *never* place your feeders inside the trap. This is highly dangerous and can cause severe injury to the swans, as once trapped, the birds are frantically looking for a way out. Anything with sharp edges can potentially hurt them, which is why we put the cushioning in to begin with.

To bait the trap, just toss a few scoopfuls of corn into it. If your trap is on land, I have found that placing a large cookie sheet (preferably a stainless steel one, which will not rust) in the center of the trap and filling it with a small amount of corn is preferable to merely throwing the corn on the ground.

After baiting, return to your vehicle and observe to see if the swans are swimming into the trap. In a couple of weeks, when they are reliably entering the trap, you can proceed with the actual trapping.

There are some very important items that you should never be without as you prepare to capture and process swans.

A good pair of waders is essential if you are trapping birds in the water. You will also need a pair for your assistant.

A scale for weighing the birds is advisable, because a bird's weight is indicative of its health. The Swan Research Program used a hanging spring–type scale and a cloth cradle. The cloth cradle was handmade of a heavy-duty fabric with rope handles on each side and large enough to hold a swan. I found this too difficult to use because the swan had to be held high in the air, swinging freely, while my helper attempted to read the numbers on the scale. I did not have the strength or the height to hold a very heavy swan that high over my head and have it clear the ground. For this reason, I purchased a baby scale that was calibrated in kilograms.

You will want to have a clipboard, paper, and sharpened pencils with you at all times for recording pertinent information. It is advisable to have a notebook or journal, as well, for recording information about your birds, their interactions with other birds, and health issues. I spent several hours each day observing and journaling in the field in all kinds of weather. I liked using the all–weather Rite in the Rain® notebooks because they were water–resistant. Always be sure to record the date and the current weather conditions. We used pre–printed data sheets when processing birds, on which the information could be easily recorded and then later transferred to computer files. A very simple data form is included at the end of this chapter.

I had sewn special wraps for containing the birds while we worked on them. One side of the wrap was made of nylon, and the other side was of a cotton canvas material. The wrap was basically a rectangle, measuring approximately 18" x 12". Two slits of equal distance were cut on the long sides, about 8" into the center. This created three flaps on each side to which VELCRO® was then attached. The VELCRO® strips should be the same length as the flap. Attach the looped VELCRO® pieces to the inside of the three flaps on one side and the fuzzy VELCRO® pieces to the outside of the three flaps on the opposite side. Finishing the seams will prevent fraying.

I also kept a plastic box with a handle, which I referred to as my banding box. Following is a list of items that I routinely kept in the box, as well as in my truck:

- A swan wrap for restraining the swan during examination and processing.
- A leg band of self–sticking VELCRO®, approximately 8" long. It is a good idea to have two of these in case one is misplaced.
- A scale for weighing and a cloth cradle if you are using a hanging scale.

- Rescue Remedy—a Bach flower essence available in natural food stores and some pharmacies.
- Alcohol and/or alcohol swabs and gauze pads—for sterilizing the dropper after administering Rescue Remedy and pads for sopping up blood in case of injuries.
- Clippers—make certain that they are good and sharp. They should be thin and pointed. They can be purchased at a fabric store or hobby supply store.
- Camera—preferably digital, for documenting birds, band numbers, and injuries or physical oddities.
- Bottled water for hydrating the bird if it is overheated and also for cleaning blood from wounds.
- Blood Stop to help coagulation in the event of bleeding.
- Hand sanitizers and wipes—especially important when pinioning young cygnets.
- Trash bags and paper towels for cleaning up poop and other trash that is produced while processing. Stressed birds often let loose of their bowels during processing. Also, when you are fitting neck and tarsus bands, sometimes the glue comes out a bit too fast.
- Large bath towels or sheets for catching and calming birds while in temporary kennels, or for providing a more sterile work area.
- Small (1/2") and larger (1") clamps for gluing tarsus and neckbands. (Optional. Needed only if you will be banding the birds.)
- If you are using plastic neckbands, you will need solvent cement glue for bonding the edges together. (Also optional.)

If you are banding birds, you will also need the appropriate number of bands. Use them in sequence, and double check to be sure that, if applying both neck and tarsus bands, the numbers match!

You will also need glue for securing plastic neckbands, as well as two sizes of clamps (large for neckbands and small for tarsus bands) to hold them in place while the glue dries. We used clear, medium-bodied solvent cement for joining acrylic. It must be quick-drying and waterproof. It is important not to leave the glue out in the heat or in very cold weather, as it is very susceptible to temperature changes. If it is too hot, it will come out too fast, and if it gets too cold, it may not come out of the tube at all. Keep the glue at room temperature, and be certain to bring it with you when trapping, in case a band has come loose and needs re-gluing. Some biologists are now using feather tags instead of bands for marking birds. Since I have no experience with these, I cannot comment on the pros and cons. I do believe that they may be more difficult to read when observing birds out in the field, especially for someone with less than perfect eyesight.

On the day that you intend to trap, you will need to unsecure the door and slide it underneath the small piece of wood that you have attached to the corner of the door. Unwind the rope and sit with the loose end of it either in your vehicle or behind a shelter where the swans cannot see you. If you are attempting to trap a pair, be certain that you have both the male and the female in the trap before you close the door. This is especially important if you are feather clipping, because if only one of the pair can fly, it causes immense stress to the pair as a unit.

I have witnessed the dire effects that feather clipping or pinioning only one half of a pair can have on their wellbeing. On one occasion, a pinioned male Trumpeter was adopted out to a new location with his partner, who could fly. The female kept flying off, causing the flightless bird severe distress, not to mention disharmony in their relationship. Eventually, the female flew off and could not be found. She returned a short time later with a Mute Swan, but disappeared again. Then her male Trumpeter partner, who was pinioned, walked off and disappeared.

More than a year later, I received a call from the adoptive pond owner, informing me that both the female and the male Trumpeter had been found at a neighboring pond some three to five miles away. Apparently, the pinioned bird had followed the streams to where his partner had flown. The owner of that pond informed me that the pair had been at her pond for at least six months, and she had been feeding them kitchen scraps.

I decided to leave the pair there for the time being, since they seemed content, although the pond did not meet requirements for proper habitat. It was regularly visited by cattle, leaving huge mud prints and uneven terrain which could have resulted in foot injuries for the swans. There were also power lines strung directly over the pond. A few weeks later I received another call from the owner, informing me that the female had flown into the power lines and died instantly. The pinioned male then wandered off alone, and I had to chase him down at another pond several miles away.

In another case, the male Trumpeter could fly, but his female partner had been pinioned. The two of them kept wandering off on foot, until finally the male flew away, deserting the female. When the male was discovered in a nearby pond, he was captured and returned to his original location near Airlie, where he formed a triad with another pair for that season. The lonely female wandered off alone and was only seen once or twice over the next couple of years. I was never able to recapture her after she had survived for more than two years alone in the wild.

If better planning had gone into the adoption of these swan pairs, these tragedies might have been prevented. For this reason, I would never consider putting a mated pair together unless both of them were either pinioned or full-winged. In the case of feather clipping, new feathers are always regrown, but this will still cause relationship problems during the period of time that one bird is flightless.

On another note, if you are trapping a family, it is essential that you get the entire family whenever possible. You must wait until the whole family is in the trap before closing the doors. This is more easily said than done, as most of the time, one or two will stand sentinel, guarding the door while the others feed. When I had a very large family to be banded and feather-clipped, I would often get only one parent and perhaps all but one juvenile. If getting the family in its entirety is too difficult, get as many as possible, and at least one of the parents. Try to get the remaining birds within a couple of days, or as soon as possible thereafter. If you are only able to get one or two birds of a large family to go into the trap on the day you are hoping to trap, *wait until another day*. You may have to try several times, but it will save you and the swans a great deal of frustration in the end. I reiterate: Trapping birds takes patience!

If you are using a one-door trap, you will want to make sure that the birds are at the closed end before pulling your trip rope. *Make certain that there are no other birds near the door that could get hit by the door on its way down*. If you are using a two-door trap, wait until the swans are in the center of the trap, again making certain that there are no birds nearby that could be hit by the doors on their way down.

Once the swan is caught, you will need at least one other person to assist you if you plan to do more than merely transport it to another location.

In most cases, swans are caught for the purpose of banding and/or feather clipping. You will want to have data sheets for recording important information, such as each swan's species, band number and/or name, weight, and sex. It is best to have several pre-made forms that can be quickly filled out as you work.

Once you have the family in the trap, go down quickly and bungee the doors closed so that they cannot be pushed open by the swans. It is always best to bungee the corners closest to the water first. You can leave the birds to calm down while you set up your work station.

You will want to set it up in the shade, if possible, especially if it is very hot outside. It also helps to have it where the bird cannot see the water while you are processing it. Once your helper or helpers have arrived (it is best if they are already there or can be there within five or ten minutes), you can walk slowly over to the trap. Remember: Always work quickly, quietly, and efficiently!

If you have trapped the swans in order to pinion, feather clip, or band them, or to examine their overall health, the following information will guide you through the processing steps.

If you have trapped the swans in order to transport them to another location, you will find tips to do so safely in Chapter IV on Safety. In most cases you will not need to know how to accomplish banding, but I have included it because I believe that the information provided can also be beneficial to biologists and interns working in the field. I believe that even a swan owner from the private sector should have a pair of long-handled snips, because if you have a swan with a band that must come off, that is what you will need for removal.

Having your work area properly arranged beforehand helps make the processing go smoothly. I have worked directly on the ground and on a portable table, but I have found that the most comfortable way to work is on top of an extra-large kennel. It seems to be about the right height for the comfort of the people working. An ideal situation is to have three people involved. The primary person will get the swans from the trap and perform all of the necessary steps in the process. The helper is there to assist; his or her main job is to have physical control over the swan at all times. If you can have a third person to be the scribe and to hand you things as needed, this is very helpful. Otherwise, two people can manage.

Have the supplies from your banding box set out for easy access, including a clipboard with blank data sheets and several sharp pencils for filling in data.

When you are ready, you and your helper can proceed to the trap. Your helper should go to the corner that is nearest the water, while you go to the closest corner. Both of you need to loosen the bungee cords, and you will open the door just enough to let yourself inside with the birds.

As soon as you are inside, the helper must move to the center of the door and use both hands and feet to keep the door closed while swans are flailing against it. He or she must pay close attention to the bottom corner closest to the water, where the swans will try to escape.

You must move slowly and purposefully toward the birds. When you have one cornered, quickly place one hand on each wing. This may take several tries, depending on how wild or how old the bird is, and also on how many birds have been caught in the trap. Pull the swan close to you until you can wrap one of your arms around its body. With your other hand, grab *both* feet. The way to do this is to place one finger between the two feet and wrap your thumb and remaining fingers around the sides. When you are certain that you have the swan secure in your arms, slowly walk toward the door of the trap, and notify your helper when you are ready to exit with the swan.

The helper must make certain that no other birds are near the door before it is opened to let you out. If there are still birds in the trap needing to be caught, the door should be opened only far enough to let you out with the bird in your arms. If other birds that are not intended to be caught are in the trap and it is certain that no others can slip out, those birds may be let out at this time.

Once you are safely out of the trap with the bird secure in your arms, the helper must re–bungee both corners of the door before following you to the work station, paying close attention to the bottom corners.

If you are trapping on land, it may be easier to throw a bath sheet over the bird you want to get hold of. I have been told by wildlife rehabilitators that they often use this method when retrieving an injured bird from the wild. If nothing else, it slows them down momentarily, which gives you an advantage.

Walk slowly to your work station, keeping the swan facing away from the water. Lay the swan on the wrap, making sure that it is facing away from the water. Simply hold the bird there until your helper joins you. At this point the primary job of the helper is to keep one hand on the wing closest to him, while you are responsible for the wing closest to you. Your assistant must keep his other hand around the swan's feet. For the remainder of the time, he is responsible for maintaining control of the bird and must not under any circumstance let go! You will immediately wrap the bird, assisted by your helper.

To use the wrap, you should have placed the nylon side down on your work station with the flaps open. Place the bird on top of the wrap, and beginning with the two middle flaps, secure them tightly around the bird by attaching the VELCRO® pieces together. Then secure the remaining four flaps by attaching the top ones in a crisscross fashion (closest to the swan's head) to the bottom ones (closest to its tail).

Once you have the bird secure in its wrap, you will need to VELCRO® its feet.

Have your helper use his arm or body to hold the wrapped bird down, while using his hands to hold one foot in each hand while you attach the VELCRO® strip around its feet. The strip of VELCRO® is first wrapped a few loops around one ankle (being sure not to wrap the tarsus band that may be on the leg) and then wrapped around both ankles, rendering the feet immobile.

Now that the bird is wrapped and its feet tied, in most cases it is easier to handle, but the helper must never let go of the swan. If it were to get away in its wraps, it could be severely injured, and of course it would also be more vulnerable to predators. I always liked to administer Rescue Remedy at this point to calm the bird down. You can open the swan's bill and squirt a few drops into its mouth, or merely rub some along the edges of its bill and into the feathers near its nostrils.

This would also be the time to check for any bleeding and injuries that the swan may have sustained while in the trap and to apply Blood Stop if needed.

The next step is to get the bird's weight. If you are using the baby scale, it should have been placed on a solid surface and zeroed out during the station set–up. (I used the open tailgate of my truck.) If you are weighing a very large bird, you may have to set the scale on something to raise it up in height, such as a cinder block, because if the swan's head or feet are touching your platform, you will not get an accurate weight. Carry the bird over to the scale and slowly let go, but keep your hands just inches above it in case it tries to jump off. Your helper can read the scale and note the weight on the data sheet. Either beforehand or immediately after you are finished with the bird, you must record the weight of the wrap (and the cloth cradle, if you are using one). Subtract that weight from the total in order to get the swan's weight. A wet wrap and cradle will weigh more than a dry one, so it is important to make this adjustment for the sake of accuracy.

If you need to sex the bird and have someone who is experienced at doing it, this would be the time to do that.

It is best to have a stool of some type or an overturned bucket on which to sit. The helper will stand behind you, holding one foot firmly in each hand, while the bird is turned upside down for examination of the sexual apparatus.

I have personally found this to be not only invasive, but quite often inaccurate. I noted several cases where birds were wrongly sexed, and their later pairings and behavior proved that they were not the sex that had originally been written in the data. Today's technology offers a much more accurate means of sexing birds through DNA analysis and, needless to say, it is far more respectful of the birds. There are companies that will do this for a nominal fee of around $25. Joy of DNA (formerly Zoogen) is a lab that performs this service. The testing may be done by drawing a small drop of blood from the tarsal vein, or by using a blood feather. If you want to do a feather pull for DNA testing, pull out the feather in a movement that is parallel to the bird's body. Also, do it quickly, as this will be less painful for the bird. There is about a 10–day turnaround for getting the results of your DNA testing.

The next step in processing the bird (and this can be done to some degree by the helper) is to make note of the bird's overall condition. You can check for rust on the head and neck, bumble feet, loose or damaged neck and tarsus bands, and any notable injuries. All pertinent information should be noted on your data sheet.

If you are going to be placing neckbands on new birds, you can begin with either the neck band or the tarsus band. If you are using plastic bands, you will want to begin by pulling the band out slightly and placing the inside edge on the outside.

Make certain that the first letter or number is at the *bottom*. This way, when you are observing a swan at a distance, through binoculars or a telescope, the number is easily read. Having the first letter or number at the bottom allows you to read it basically from left to right.

You will need to pull the band out again to gently slip it over the ankle, in the case of the tarsus band, or over the swan's neck, if it is a neckband. Your helper will need to steady the swan's neck and may have to help push it very gently to fit inside the band. Double check to be sure that the inside edge is out. Place a thin line of glue along the dark edge and spread it around with your finger. (This is where having a few paper towels comes in handy.) Then pull the band out again to reposition the edge back to the inside. Slide the band up and down the swan's neck (or leg) a few times to be certain that it is not too tight and adjust in or out as necessary. Apply a clamp to both edges of the neckband and allow the glue a few minutes to dry. Be certain that the swan is able to rest its head on your working platform, as the weight of the clamps puts too much stress on the neck otherwise. While you allow the neckband to dry, you can proceed with the tarsus band (or vice versa). You will need a smaller clamp for the tarsus bands. I have found that the type of plastic clip that you would use on a bag of potato chips to keep them fresh works quite well. If you are attaching the much smaller U.S. Fish and Wildlife Service metal bands (tarsus only), they can be opened slightly and then retightened with small, pointed pliers.

One last thing that you will want to decide upon prior to attaching a tarsus band is on which leg you intend to place it. At the Swan Research Program, we always placed the plastic tarsus band on the right leg of a *known–age* bird. If we did not know the bird's age, or if there was already a metal FWS band on the right leg, then we would place it on the left tarsus.

Once you have completed the banding and have checked to be certain that the glue has dried, you may either release the bird or proceed to the final step of feather clipping, if needed.

I need to point out that when you are working around the birds, always walk *behind* and not in front of them. They should also be facing *away* from the water for the duration of the processing. It is very important that you keep talking to a minimum. Do not speak loudly or make sudden movements.

As a rule, we always clipped males on the right side and females on the left side. If you have not sexed the bird and are unsure, sometimes you can guess by the weight whether a bird is male or female. In general, the cob is larger than the pen. If it is a Mute Swan, the knob on the cob is generally larger as well. Once you have determined on which side you wish to do the feather clipping, you may need to switch sides with your helper.

Up to this point, your helper should have had both hands on

the swan the entire time. If you need to switch, move around *behind* the swan to your helper's side and hold the swan (wings and feet) while your helper walks around *behind* the swan to the other side. When your helper once again has hold of the swan, you will need to re-wrap the swan so that the wing to be clipped is *outside* the wrap. Do this gently and carefully, being sure that the feathers are smoothed underneath the wrap.

At this point the helper will need to use mostly his or her body to apply pressure to the swan's body, keeping hold of the feet with one hand, and with the other hand holding the joint of the wing that is to be clipped. It is very important that the wing be held straight out. If the wing is raised too high, it can cause injury! If the swan struggles and tries to raise its wing, you must stop momentarily, pressing the wing back to the swan's side until it becomes calm again. Some swans are completely calm and cooperative during this process, but more often than not, the bird will squirm and you will have to keep beginning again.

If your helper has been holding the swan for several moments, he or she may become very uncomfortable. As a helper, your back may start to ache from bending over, your hand may hurt from holding the feet, or you may get an itch that you want to scratch, but under no circumstances are you to let go of the swan. If you must let go for a moment, first tell the person who is doing the clipping, so that she may hold the swan while you stretch or stand for a moment. Or get another person to relieve you. Never, ever let go of the swan in this situation!

Before you begin the feather clipping, you first want to be sure that molting has been completed and the feathers have hardened. Observing the swans every day, or at least several times a week, will help you determine this ahead of time before you actually trap the birds. If you have already caught the bird and realize too late that it is too soon to feather clip, you will have to release it and try again in a couple of weeks.

The quill should be hard and white, and you should not be able to see blood in the quill. If you cut one feather and it begins to bleed, that is evidence that it is too soon. Apply Blood Stop, and when you are certain that the bleeding has been controlled, release the bird back into the water.

The purpose of feather clipping is, of course, to maintain the bird in a flightless condition. For aesthetic purposes, we generally left the first primary feather intact and sometimes the first two primaries. Clipping the remaining nine primaries will usually suffice. However, if the swans are still attaining airlift, you may want to go ahead and clip two of the secondary feathers as well. Your clippers should be good and sharp for a clean cut. As you cut each one, do so as near to the top of the feather as possible, keeping the smaller feathers and the down out of the way. Your cuts should be straight and not at an angle. Your helper can assist you in counting, because when the swans are feisty and difficult, it is easy to lose count. If you both forget, simply count the feathers that are already on the ground. (Be sure to pick them up in between birds.)

Releasing was always my favorite part of trapping birds. I believe this is because I felt so terrible about having first "tricked" them into going into the trap and then causing them the stress of being captured and processed. It was much worse, of course, when I had to feather clip them. It was my job and I was forced to comply with federal and state agencies that demanded it, but I had a hard time forgiving myself for doing it. These birds have been born with the ability to fly, and I do not feel that we humans have the right to take that from them. It always seemed ironic to me that the birds I cared for were there because Bill Sladen wished them to relearn the migration route. But how are they supposed to learn when they are not even allowed to fly?! I intend to spend the remainder of my life fighting for their freedom.

Let's return now to the final step of trapping, which is the release.

Carefully unwrap the bird. The person who is going to do the release must get hold of the bird securely in her arms, with one arm holding the wings tight against the body and her other hand holding the feet securely. The other person can then remove the VELCRO® from the bird's feet.

Walk slowly down to the water, making sure that the bird is facing *away* from the water. The bird will most likely try to jump from your arms, so it is very important to hold onto the bird until you are ready to release it, or you may cause injury to the bird or to yourself. Walk a few feet out into the water and set the bird down without letting go, now *facing* the water. Wait for the bird to calm down and, as you let go, turn your face away from the bird. The bird will flap its wings as it makes its getaway, so you want to keep your face out of harm's way. That is, you do not want to be struck by the bird's wing as it is coming down.

When the bird is safely back in the water, you will need to watch it for a few minutes to ensure that it drinks water and is not showing any signs of distress.

When you have no more birds to retrieve from the trap, you may open the doors so that any remaining birds that may have been caught in there can swim out. Prop the door (or doors) up, making sure that it is (they are) secure.

You may leave your doors propped up and your trap intact for a few weeks until you have completed all the trapping that you need to do.

I do not recommend leaving the doors up indefinitely, because they will become warped over time and will not close properly. The fence panels will rust and the plastic zip ties will become dry and brittle and eventually break off and fall into the water. As I said earlier, it can be very dangerous for the swans if the zip ties are accidentally ingested.

The bungee cords may be left on the panels while you are still trapping, but they also become weathered in a short amount of time, eventually snapping and breaking.

Sample Data Form

S
W
A
N

S A N C T U A R Y

Educating One Pond Owner at a time...

Data Form

Date_____   Owner_____

Species _____   Name_____

Sex   Female_____   Male _____   Unknown_____

Weight _____   Kilograms _____   Pounds

Neck Band # _____   Tarsus Band #_____

FWS Metal Band # _____   Wing Tag #_____

Hatch Year_____   Age_____

Pinioned   Yes_____ No_____ Left Side_____ Right Side_____

Full-Winged   Yes_____ No_____   Captured Alive   Yes_____   No_____

Capture Method (Trap, Hand, Net, Boat) _____

Capture Location_____

Re-located?   Yes_____ No_____ To_____

_____

Necropsy Performed?   Yes_____ No_____ Cause of Death_____

Notes

CHAPTER VII

CARE THROUGH THE SEASONS

Winter

I begin this chapter with the winter season because it is the least active time for the swans, although it is unlikely that this is the time of year when you will acquire them. Perhaps I should have put this chapter at the beginning, so that those needing immediate information would find it right away, but I have presented the chapters so that answers to particular questions may be found quickly when there is an urgent need. I have often repeated information in more than one chapter because of its importance. Although I would be pleased to have you read it through from cover to cover, I also realize that this type of manual is often consulted for specific answers to specific questions, and I sincerely hope that it will be able to serve you in this manner.

Winter is a great time to photograph your swans and to simply enjoy them. It is also a time when you must be diligent about monitoring their health and daily activity.

When *December* rolls around, it is important to observe your swans every single day to ensure that they have not succumbed to illness or injury.

Maintain the cleanliness of the feeders, and if any ice has formed around them, you will need to get into the water in your waders and use your feet to break it up. If freezing is a frequent problem, you may want to relocate the feeders so that they receive direct sunlight during this time of year. This is important, because when feeding, the swans take a mouthful of food and drop it into the water; they then eat it from the pond floor, taking up sufficient water along with the food. If there is no open water around the feeder, they can choke or aspirate the dry food.

Also, when considering the placement of your feeders, have them turned away from prevailing winds to prevent rain and snow from wetting the food.

You will save yourself a lot of time and trouble down the road if you pay attention to these things and stay ahead of potential problems.

Throughout the winter months, it is important to check on the swans immediately after a particularly dangerous storm. If a swan is injured or sick, the sooner you make the discovery, the sooner you can take steps to get it to a veterinarian, or at least to ease its suffering if death is imminent.

A bird with a foot injury can become stuck out on the ice with no way to escape predators.

One winter, a Mute Swan that I was caring for became lodged out on the ice. He was an older swan and had become crippled and unable to walk. While he was sleeping during the night, the water froze around him and he could not get himself back to the water. I had to go out in the boat, painstakingly breaking the ice as I went, before I could reach him. At last I was able to free him by opening up a small channel of open water. Unfortunately, this swan died a few months later, and his partially eaten body was found near the edge of the pond. The owners, who had enjoyed their swan for several years, were devastated and resisted my offer to provide them with another swan.

January will be your least busy time of year in the overall care of your swans, and in many ways, it can be the most enjoyable. If you live within range of the annual migration, you will be able to observe the comings and goings of other birds to your pond. If at all possible, you should have a spotting scope set up in a window overlooking your pond, so that you can quickly identify other species.

If you have excellent habitat, you may have a slew of avian visitors, including several duck species. I would often get back in my truck after filling feeders for the swans and sit there for a few minutes. Several ducks, such as the ring–necked ducks and buffleheads, would generally come over to the feeders once I had left, or if I was in my truck and they could not see me. I was then able to watch them from a very short distance. The diving ducks are especially fun to watch. This is an excellent time to photograph birds on the ice, and you can even do this under a full moon!

Regular monitoring of your swans is essential at this time of year. It is imperative that the swans have open water around their feeders. This may require that you go out and manually break ice from around the feeder. The swans can still feed from it, but they will be vulnerable to predation should another animal come after them while they are on the ice.

Keep a close eye on your swans, especially during and after a brutal winter storm. Look regularly for any signs of poor health or injuries. A swan that continually holds its mouth open is probably sick.

Make note of the overall condition and weight of your swans and whether or not proper preening is being done. Preening is a very important part of a swan's daily existence. The swan uses oil from the uropygial gland, which is located above the base of the tail, to waterproof its feathers. It becomes life threatening if the swan is unable to waterproof itself and becomes wet.

Make certain that feeders are maintained to prevent disease and that they are always filled. Swans eat every few hours, so it is important that their feeders not become empty when other food sources are not available.

Toward the end of *February*, your swans will begin pairing off, and you may notice fighting and changes in partners. Established pairs may be displaced by a younger pair.

It was not uncommon for me to find one or more dead swans at this time of year as a result of fighting. I witnessed a fight firsthand in which the instigator was floating in the water moments after the fight had ceased. When I walked out into the water to check on him, I found that he was dead. A few days later, I arrived to fill the feeders and saw another male's body washed up at the edge of the shore. The death had probably occurred not more than a few hours prior to my arrival. These two birds were healthy. Their deaths were due to the overcrowding at the reservoir and the influx of hormones in the birds at this time of year.

If you have not already done so, this is the time to begin cleaning off the islands. Dead grasses, shrubs, and vines from the previous year need to be cut back to ensure ease of access for the swans when they begin nest building. The debris can be cut into smaller twigs and piled near the nest site if there is an existing nest from the previous year. Toward the end of the month, straw may also be brought out and set near the nest. If you have only a raft and not an island, it will be necessary to provide plenty of straw or other nesting material if you hope to have the swans build a nest on it.

You will also want to ensure that breeding swans have adequate nutrition at this time. We made a practice of mixing Purina® Layena® nuggets with the corn to assist them with their egg production. Continue feeding the Layena until the swan begins laying her eggs, which generally happens around mid- to late April, depending on the species, the specific pair, and the weather.

I noted in my own observations that a couple of the pairs that had lost several cygnets in a previous year (probably due to snapping turtle attacks) nested earlier the following year. I wondered if perhaps this was a means of keeping their young safe before the snapping turtles became active. It is certainly a phenomenon deserving more study and observation. For this reason, it is important to keep track of several pairs—their date of laying, the date incubation begins, and the date of hatch—in addition to the number of surviving cygnets and the weather trends for that specific year. Keep these records for several consecutive years. You may be surprised at how often you will refer back to them, and your notes and observations may prove valuable at some point in the future.

Spring

Depending on where you live, toward the end of *March*, you will want to begin removing the deicers. Be sure to clean them up, check for any damage, especially to the electrical cord, and then store them after they are completely dry. If a deicer is still under warranty, it is also helpful to make a note of its serial number and a note of where it was used, and then store it in its original box.

The parent swans will probably begin to kick out the young from the previous year, and you may have to intervene at this point and move the juveniles to another location. It really depends on the parents. Some are more tolerant and will allow the juveniles to remain nearby, but as their custodian, you will need to have a plan for dealing with whatever situation you encounter.

If you are encouraging your swans to nest, you may want to put out more straw on the islands and the rafts, especially if you see that the swans are preparing to make a nest. Once they begin, they should not be disturbed.

It is fun to watch them in this undertaking. Usually the male will pull up mosses and other submerged plants from the bottom of the pond, near the edge of the island. He lays them there, and then the female carries this material over and adds it to her nest, along with grasses, sedges, twigs, cattails, and the straw that you may have provided, or other plant materials that she finds to her liking.

Most waterfowl that have reached sexual maturity will begin pairing off in the early spring. If you observe them, you may notice their brief sexual encounters that take place in the water, followed by bathing and much wing flapping. Ducks and Canada geese begin nesting a few weeks to a month earlier than the swans. Swans will use the same nest year after year, building it higher and higher.

Canada geese will often use one of these swan nests to lay their own eggs. This presents a problem, because the female goose will still be incubating her eggs when the female swan is ready to nest. The swan will evict the goose from her nest, and she may push out the goose eggs; more often, she will lay her own eggs right next to the goose eggs. Swans lay approximately one egg every other day and do not begin incubating until all the eggs have been laid. If there are goose eggs remaining in her nest, they will begin to spoil, and therefore need to be removed. At other times, the Canada goose may lay her eggs in a nest of her own creation, but if it is too near the swan's territory, the swan will chase off the goose, disrupting incubation, and quite often will kill any goslings that have hatched.

At Swan Sanctuary, I had a pair of Canada geese that nested on the island for the two springs that I lived there. I named them Rose and Rambo.

Rose was sweet, but Rambo was a formidable protector. He kept chasing one of my older male swans up into the corner and would not allow him in the water.

The following year, after the male swan had died, I had a female, Henrietta, who was alone. She got along splendidly with Rambo and Rose and often sat next to Rose on the island. After the goslings hatched, she would follow the family around and help to protect them. It was so sweet. My island was quite small, not much bigger than a full-size mattress. One day I noticed Henrietta, Rose, and a great blue heron all on the island together, but one got off before I could snap a picture.

One of the things that I loved most about observing the swans was making note of the interactions between species. It was very common to see a cormorant sitting on a raft or island next to an incubating Canada goose. It is a common practice for pond owners to put swan decoys in a pond to keep the Canada geese away, but in my experience, the swans and the Canada geese get along just fine for the most part.

April begins a much busier time for the swans and will require diligence on the part of the caretakers.

By now, if you have more than one nesting pair, you should have determined the locations of the nests and have begun regular monitoring of the nesting pairs. The nests are really quite remarkable to see. Generally, the mother pulls down from her breast and uses it to line her nest.

You will want to do nest checks once the pen begins laying her eggs. You can also stop supplementing with the Layena. If she is still getting off the nest frequently, she has probably not finished laying her clutch. She will lay approximately one egg every other day until all of her eggs have been deposited in the nest. When she does get off the nest, she will carefully cover and hide her eggs, so you may have to dig down into the straw to find them. The cob will often remain near the nest and defend it while she is off feeding, so be sure to take along a broom should it become necessary to defend yourself from him. Count the eggs as soon as possible when you believe that she has finished laying them and *keep accurate and thorough notes.* Also, when you are certain that she has begun incubating, make a note of the date so that you will know the expected day of hatching.

Remember, too, if a Canada goose has used the nest, you will need to remove any remaining goose eggs.

If you do not wish to have the swans successfully nest, such as in the case of Mute Swans, you can go out and destroy the nest before the pen has the opportunity to lay her eggs. She will probably try to rebuild it, but once the hormones in her body begin to decrease, she will eventually give up nesting for the year. If you choose to destroy any eggs that she has laid, you have a few options. If taken fresh, right after they have been laid, you may use the eggs for cooking or making an omelet. I personally have never eaten a swan egg and I never could, but apparently they are quite good.

Making Nest Checks of Breeding Swans

You may also choose to oil or addle the eggs, but this requires careful timing and a certain amount of work.

You will need to check with the U.S. Fish and Wildlife Service and your local state agency to see if a special permit is required. Plan to apply for any necessary permits at least two months before you anticipate needing to do the addling.

There are six stages in the development of an egg. If you are planning to oil the eggs, this can be done anytime during the first through the fourth stage. If you are shaking the eggs, you will need to wait until the egg is in the second or third stage. Once it has evolved into the fourth stage and beyond, it is getting too late in the development, and you will need to allow the mother to continue incubating. Please refer to the chart below, which depicts the six stages of egg development.

Before heading out in your boat to do your nest check, you will need to have a few supplies. Also, it is helpful if you have another person who can use a small broom to defend you from attack. If possible, wait until the mother gets off the nest to feed, as this will buy you a little time and cause less stress for the nesting pair.

Stages of Egg Development

Flotation Chart

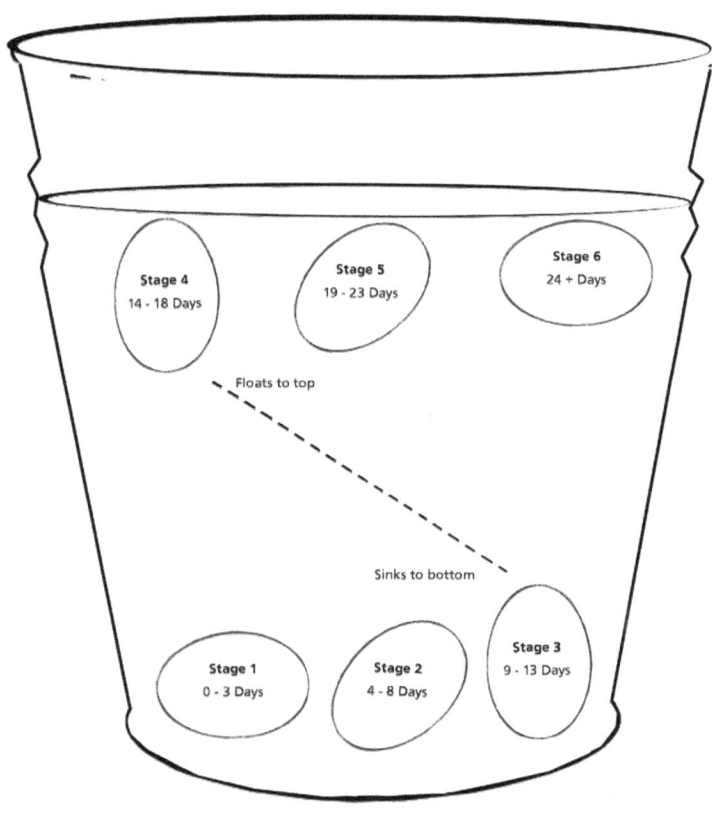

Stage 4
14 - 18 Days

Stage 5
19 - 23 Days

Stage 6
24 + Days

Floats to top

Sinks to bottom

Stage 1
0 - 3 Days

Stage 2
4 - 8 Days

Stage 3
9 - 13 Days

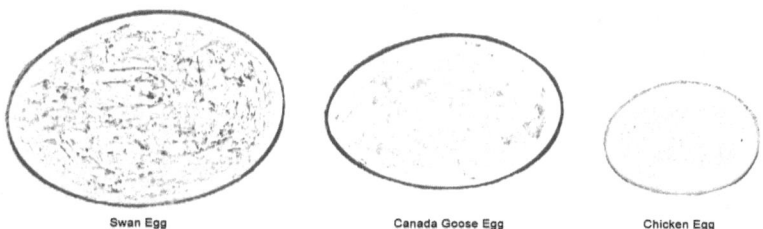

Swan Egg   Canada Goose Egg   Chicken Egg

Egg Size Comparisons

Take a bucket, an egg flotation chart (see above), and a data sheet and pencil for recording the number of eggs, their stage of development, and your actions. The type of oil approved for addling eggs is corn oil, which may be taken in a small spray bottle.

If the eggs are still cool, the mother has not begun incubating yet. You can check back in about a week.

If the eggs are warm, fill your bucket with water. Float each egg from the nest in the bucket of water, one at a time, making note of the stage. Then replace it in the same position that you found it. If you are oiling the eggs, you may spray the entire clutch at once, covering the top two–thirds of the egg. The oil penetrates the pores in the shell, causing asphyxiation to the embryo. If you choose to shake the eggs, be certain that they are at stage two, or preferably at stage three. Shake each one vigorously until you can hear sloshing of the embryo from within the egg. Replace the eggs exactly as you found them and cover them back over with any nesting material that the mother may have used to hide them.

After the eggs have been oiled or addled, you will need to return to the nest after two weeks. Retrieve the eggs from the nest and bury them. This is very important, because if the mother continues to sit and incubate the eggs, she will use up her energy reserves and her health will be compromised.

As spring progresses, you should begin to see the SAV (submerged aquatic vegetation) beginning to grow. At Airlie, we had an abundance of *Potamogeton crispus* for a couple of months; then as it began to die off, the *Hydrilla* and the duckweed would emerge. Once there is a good supply of these natural foods, you can decrease and completely stop supplemental feeding for the summer.

In the spring, it is wonderful to photograph a pair building their nest or the pen sitting on her nest. Do be aware that the cob will be sitting close to his mate while she is incubating, and he will guard the nest whenever she gets off to feed, generally a couple of times a day. She will also bury the eggs prior to getting off the nest to deter would–be predators. I advise having a small broom with you whenever you are out doing your nest checks, as the cobs can be extremely aggressive at this time.

It would be a treat to get photos of cygnets just emerging from their eggs, as long as it could be done without disturbing them, such as with a camera trap. The pen will protect her newly hatched babies underneath her expansive wings, so when you see her holding her wings out from her body, this is a sure sign that the eggs are hatching.

I recently found a wonderful clip on YouTube that was created by the Abbotsbury Swannery in England. It depicts the hatching of Mute Swan eggs, and I recommend watching it. Here is a link to the clip, which is four and a half minutes long. https://www.youtube.com/watch?v=qJa8Tp7xBD4

I especially love taking pictures of the cygnets as they dive and upend themselves. It is no surprise that swans have been loved for millennia and have been the object of art and stories for generations.

Summer

May and *June* are an exciting time in the world of swans as cygnets hatch and you get to see the proud parents swimming across the lake with as many as seven cygnets between them. Generally the mother is in the lead and the father follows along at the end of the procession.

This can also be the most vulnerable time, as you may see cygnets one day and none the next. In spite of diligent parents, newly hatched cygnets can easily fall prey to predators. At Airlie, we lost more offspring to snapping turtles than to all other causes combined. One proven pair of breeders had hatched five cygnets in 2010, and in five days' time, there was not a single one remaining. This particular pond had numerous snapping turtles. Only a few weeks before their disappearance, one of the volunteers had witnessed a snapping turtle attacking and killing the goslings of a Canada geese pair. She said that it appeared to be killing them merely because it could and did not even eat them.

Depending on the species you are caring for, you may have cygnets by the middle of *May* or earlier. The trumpeters that I cared for at Airlie would generally begin incubating eggs by the beginning of *June*.

I must reiterate that it is very important to the research to keep good records. Make note of the dates of laying, incubating, and hatching, how many cygnets hatch, and how many survive. Was it an especially hard winter? Does your pond have snapping turtles or other predators? If the eggs or the cygnets are the victims of predators, it is important to discover what killed them and how, so you can take steps to eliminate this problem the following year. Keeping records for several years in a row will indicate if a particular pair begins breeding close to the same day as the previous year. If they breed earlier or later in some years, your detailed notes can be used to help you understand the reasons why.

Once the cygnets have hatched, the parents will often lead them to feed in an area where duckweed and other pond weeds are growing just on top of the surface of the water. You may want to supplement the swan's feed with Purina® Start & Grow® to provide them with added nutrition.

We used to mix it in with the corn, but much of it was wasted, especially after a heavy rain, when it would tend to get mushy. I later discovered that if I placed a small amount of it on a large stainless steel cookie sheet and placed the sheet just at the edge of the shore, the cygnets benefited more from it.

If you know that you will need to trap the family later on to band them, you can get them accustomed early on to going into a trap to feed. Just make certain that if you feed them inside a trap, both doors are open so that they can escape any would–be predators.

Remember that if you are planning to pinion the cygnets, it needs to be done at two weeks of age. When you trap the family, you will need to separate the cygnets from the parents and work as quickly as possible. I highly advise you to find someone who has experience doing this. After each cygnet has been pinioned and you have ensured that the bleeding has stopped, return it immediately to its parents.

When *July* rolls around, you should be able to discontinue supplemental feeding as long as there is plenty of SAV growing in the pond. The feeders should be removed, cleaned, sterilized, and stored for the season.

Continue to monitor the families and make a note of when the parents and non–paired juveniles and adults begin their molt. It takes about 30 days to complete their molt. Generally, the female will molt first when you have a breeding pair.

Once the new feathers have grown out to where they are even with the tail feathers, it is probably safe to feather clip, if this is what you need to do. The quill should be hardened and you should not be able to see blood in the quill. If you see blood and/or the quill is still too soft, do not attempt to feather clip, as loss of blood will endanger the bird's health. There is a fine line to catching them at just the right time. If you wait too long, you risk having them fly off before you can get them feather clipped. This happened with one of our reliable breeding pairs. They had been displaced by a younger, stronger pair, and as soon as their feathers were regrown, they split in search of new territory. This is, of course, Nature's way.

In a case where a territory is not threatened and the birds are not migratory, they will not venture too far from their established area. Young juveniles will stay at their parents' sides during the winter months, so feather clipping them is not really necessary. I personally feel that it is important to allow the birds at least some flight, as it helps to build strength and breast muscle. It also allows them the freedom to seek out suitable food sources in the area, which they instinctively know provides the necessary nutrition for their optimum health.

Having cared for the swan collection as long as I did, I was able to observe marked differences between the birds that had been captive for most or all of their lives and those that had managed to escape being feather clipped. Five Trumpeters from the 2009 hatch year had managed to escape being feather clipped. The biologist who was in charge of the collection prior to my taking it over had never succeeded in capturing these birds. They were kept at an estate about 35 miles north of Airlie. They never flew much farther away than a few miles and always returned to their home. They were large and healthy and had enormous breasts, while the captive swans at Airlie were thin and emaciated.

Also during *July*, you can begin setting up traps if you have not already done so. Begin baiting at least two weeks prior to the time that you intend to trap birds to get them accustomed to swimming through the traps. By mid– to late *August*, at least some of the birds should be ready to be feather clipped, if this is what you must do. Hopefully, all you will be required to do is to band them in order to keep track of them.

It is best if you have at least two trained assistants when the time comes for trapping; however, I was often left with no other choice but to train people on the fly and hope for the best. Once, when I had asked someone who was completely green to hold the door while I went into the trap after the swan, he did not hold the bottom corner and the swan managed to escape. I finally caught the swan again a few weeks later, but it created unnecessary stress to the bird. It is sometimes helpful to use a decoy in the trap if you are having trouble getting the birds to go in. I purchased decoys from Knutson's Sporting Goods, in Michigan.

Since it can be very hot this time of year, try to set up your work station in the shade to minimize the stress on the birds. Remember to work quickly and quietly and in an organized fashion to help the process go as smoothly as possible. Trap early in the day before the heat intensifies. The birds are generally more interested in feeding early in the day, as well, tending to want to sleep and rest in the afternoon heat.

Autumn

Your swans will have spent the past two months feeding voraciously. The cygnets will have attained the same size as the adults in only three to four months, though as juveniles they will maintain their grey plumage for a year or longer. In the wild, this is in preparation for the long journey ahead of them. I would often see great white egrets fishing next to the swans in late summer and early autumn. They would congregate in large flocks to put on the necessary weight in preparation for their imminent migration. I love to see the intermingling of different bird species. It is a beautiful model for how humans of different races might get along for the good of all.

Continue to monitor the presence of SAV. By late *September*, depending on the climate where you live, you may want to resume supplemental feeding. In most areas, the SAV will be mostly diminished by the end of *October*. Make certain that your feeders have been thoroughly cleaned and sterilized before you begin filling them again. Also, be sure to make any necessary repairs to the feeders. This is a good time to begin installing deicers, before the weather gets too cold and the water begins to freeze. When the SAV is no longer growing, begin supplemental feeding again. Keep an eye on how much the swans are eating so that the food does not become moldy and to cut down on waste. It is best to check the feeders at least twice a week; more frequently would not hurt.

You should have all your deicers and rafts in place by the end of *October*. I once had to break through ice in a canoe to reach the float and attach the deicer in very cold weather, so I learned this lesson the hard way. Plunging your fingers into ice–cold water to attach chains is no picnic, so prepare for cold weather well in advance of it.

In early *November*, you will want to begin looking out for wild birds flying into or through your area.

This is one of the most exciting times of year, as Tundra Swans fly over in their winter migration. The sound of them will often be the first thing to draw your attention to them. You will want to keep track of individuals with neck bands, of families, and of any unusual birds, such as a leusistic bird. This term refers to birds with naturally occurring variations, such as orange or yellow or other colored legs and/or bills.

Be sure to make note of any Trumpeters that may be flying in with groups of Tundras. If you observe either of these phenomena or observe banded swans flying in from another area, please report it to The Trumpeter Swan Society or to Swan Sanctuary, as this is valuable to ongoing research. In the case of banded swans, be sure to note the color and the number of the neck and/or tarsus bands. These notes are vitally important, especially when you compare one year to another and if you have specific birds or families that return year after year.

It is really fun to watch the other waterfowl species that may visit your pond as well. The diving ducks are a joy to watch. It is best to observe either from your vehicle or from a blind, so that the birds will not be frightened and will come closer to the shore.

I cannot stress enough the importance of maintaining a journal. Any unusual findings can be reported to The Trumpeter Swan Society and to the National Audubon Society. This is also a great time to photograph the birds, especially if you have the privilege of witnessing wild Tundra Swans on migration.

CHAPTER VIII
CONCLUSION

The Future of Swans

Swans have been revered throughout history and integrated into many cultural myths and stories. Their beauty is undeniable, and the extinction of even one of the species would be a devastating loss.

It is the density of their bones, which are supported by inner struts within an air cavity, instead of marrow, that gives these magnificent birds the ability to fly. Their bones are strong and stiff, enabling them to migrate for long distances. Flutes carved from ancient Mute Swan wing bones were recently discovered in Germany. These flutes are more than 35,000 years old and are said to produce a hauntingly beautiful sound. But it is the beauty of these birds in our midst that we must strive to preserve, not their final remains.

If you are a property owner with a pond and have contemplated the possibility of obtaining swans, I sincerely hope that this book has provided you with enough information on which to base your decision, for certainly it is not one to be made lightly.

It is important that you understand that swans are not pets. Unlike your dog or cat, or even your typical farm animal, swans are unique, and more important, they are wild. The responsibility of caring for them should be carefully weighed before investing your money and time in them.

Too many animals suffer as a direct result of our human ignorance. As with so many other species, swans are facing loss of habitat, diminishing food sources, and a barrage of toxins in our environment. Perils are encountered every day from power lines, from lead, and from trash left strewn everywhere. We have altered our planet so drastically that many species have been lost forever. With so much of their history in legends and in art, it would be a tragedy indeed if we were to lose swans forever.

It is only through knowledge and understanding that we can change our perceptions and our behavior to accommodate species other than our own and to create hope not only for their survival, but also for an existence in which they can thrive and flourish. It is my hope, through this book and through Swan Sanctuary, to inform and to educate the public—one pond owner at a time.

I would like to end with a bit more information about Swan Sanctuary.

The business was set up initially as a sole proprietorship, rather than as a 501(c)(3). I believe that I can better provide for the swans by working for profit, not as a nonprofit. I worked for many years for the nonprofit organization Swan Research Program and for Environmental Studies on the Piedmont. I also recently worked for a short period at a cat shelter. I saw firsthand many of the problems that nonprofits face. Their biggest challenge is uncertainty of income. They have a constant need to write grant applications and to come up with innovative ideas to solicit donations and maintain their tax–free status. To me, this represents a poverty mindset, and I personally have no problem paying taxes. I do believe that current tax loopholes are responsible for much unfairness and deceit by the very wealthy, and I also realize that if it were not for taxes, our lives would be seriously lacking. We must be grateful each day for those things that are provided for us on a regular basis and to which we give little acknowledgement.

After I had taken over care of the swan collection at Airlie (and to some degree when I was working merely as a volunteer), I personally witnessed a great deal of waste and disregard for even very costly items.

The nursery that had been used for the original ultra–light experiment had fallen into complete disrepair. After I had begun trying to replace some of the items, I discovered that some of them were quite expensive. I found numerous aerators that had not been properly cared for or stored during the off season, so that the motors were burned out and the cords had been chewed by muskrats. Rebar, fence panels, and feeders had fallen into the water and were then left and forgotten about. Rowboats had missing oars or only one oar. I was appalled at the waste of resources by the organization, even while it continued to complain about lack of money.

The problem that arises when you have to use volunteers is that they are not always reliable. Quite often the volunteers merely want a signature stating that they have done so many hours of volunteer work to attach to their résumés. Very rarely do they actually have a vested interest in the work they are doing or in the organization itself.

Shelter animals often have to eat what is provided for free; it is cheap and is therefore nutritionally inadequate and may contain dangerous chemical additives and food colorings. I believe that if we are going to take on the challenge of caring for any species, then we must also do it in the most responsible manner possible. As a for-profit sanctuary, I can provide superior supplemental feeding for the swans, rather than having to resort to giving them corn that has been grown for cattle. Corn is to swans what junk food and fast food are to humans. It provides little nutritive value and basically serves only to fill their stomachs.

I want to provide the best and the finest possible care for these birds and not have to settle for less than ideal conditions. This means providing for them the habitat and food that most closely mimic what they would have in the wild and what their bodies are designed to eat. If we introduce our own chemical-laden and genetically modified (GMOs) foods to them, we make them susceptible to all kinds of unknown diseases. The ideal of any animal sanctuary should be to provide and maintain the quality of life for that species that is inherent to it.

Swan Sanctuary works directly with nonprofit businesses, so if it were operating as a nonprofit as well, it would be in direct competition with those businesses on which it relies. For this reason, I will use every means possible to make profits with and for Swan Sanctuary. I believe that in functioning this way, I can do a greater service for the swans. While working as an independent contractor, I have the opportunity to educate one pond owner at a time and to be an effective advocate for our North American swan species.

Should I reach the point where the sanctuary is making a profit above and beyond its operating needs, I intend to use surplus profits to buy more land with ponds and lakes and use it to return habitat to those species from which it has been taken—

as well as perhaps to Native Americans who are willing to provide good stewardship of the land.

My vision for the future of the sanctuary is to have several acres of prime wetland with multiple ponds and lakes. I will provide blinds for those who wish to quietly observe the swans, and I will provide talks and presentations to those wishing to know and learn more about swans, ponds, and wetland habitats. There will be a minimal fee for these services. I also plan to have an on-site and an online store for selling swan art and swan-related items.

I hope to carry on with my own personal study of swans—in particular their vocal and non-vocal modes of communication. I used to love listening to the parents "talk" to their cygnets, and I would love the opportunity to learn more about their vocalizations. The communication between mated pairs and the larger flocks is fascinating as well.

With enough caring individuals who are willing to learn, I believe that we can bring swans back to a state of grace. This book is one step toward that goal.

RESOURCES

Floating Islands

BioHaven® Floating Island available from
www.martinecosystems.com

Feeders

Pet Lodge Chow Hound available at
www.walmart.com
www.tractorsupply.com
www.valleyvet.com
www.amazon.com
and most feed and pet supply stores

Scales

www.oldwillknottscales.com for both hanging–style and baby scales

Decoys

www.knutsondecoys.com
www.rogerssportinggoods.com

Aerators

www.airolator.com
www.thepondguy.com
www.otterbine.com

Journals

Rite in the Rain®
www.riteintherain.com

Waders

www.sportsmansguide.com
Cabela's, www.cabelas.com
Bass Pro Shops®, www.basspro.com
Also available at most sporting goods stores and www.amazon.com

DNA Sexing

Joy of DNA, www.joyofdna.com (formerly Zoogen.com)

Fabric

Polyester cut–to–fit air conditioning filter rolls can be obtained from any air conditioning supply house or an online supplier. They come in various sizes, but 36–48" width x 30' length x 1" thickness is best.

Glue

We used Weld–On® clear, medium–bodied solvent cement for joining acrylic. www.weldon.com
Their product may no longer be available in tube form. This glue needs to be strong, clear, medium–bodied, and fast drying for joining acrylic. It can also be found at www.ellsworth.com

Organizations

The Trumpeter Swan Society
www.trumpeterswansociety.org

The Trumpeter Swan Fund
www.trumpeterswanfund.org

Wyoming Wetlands Society
www.wyomingwetlandssociety.org

ABOUT THE AUTHOR

Lisbeth Williams believes that work and play should be inextricably intertwined, because life is too short to work at an uninspiring job that masks our true purpose.

She has approached with passion everything that she has done in her own life, beginning with giving birth at home to her three daughters.

As a single mother, after completing an aesthetics course, she developed her own skin care business. In addition, she completed three years of study in The Science of Mind, and later, a course from The Institute of Children's Literature. Her story "My New Year's Garden" appeared in the *GreenPrints* Winter 2002–03 issue. It was nominated for a Garden Globe Award. In 2005 she completed Master Gardener training, creating four brochures as part of her required hours. She went on to complete the Master Naturalist course in 2008.

After her girls had left home, she pursued her dream of living in the country and having swans. She began volunteering for The Swan Research Program in Warrenton, Virginia in 2005, where she was eventually hired as a contractor/consultant to care for the collection of over 70 swans. There she conceived and then implemented the idea for Swan Sanctuary.

The sanctuary, which is a sole proprietorship, is currently at a temporary location near Denver, Colorado. Lisbeth is seeking to relocate to the Northwest, where she can better serve our native swans.

She provides free swan consulting services through her

website, www.swansanctuary.org, and continues to write and garden.

Email: Lisbeth@swansanctuary.org

Telephone: 540-395-9822

ABOUT THE ILLUSTRATOR

Sandra Davis is a Denver artist and illustrator specializing in animal portraiture. To learn more about her work and for contact information, please visit her website: www.SandraDavisArt.com

EDITING AND PUBLISHING ASSISTANCE

This book was proofread and edited by David and Leonore Dvorkin, of Denver, Colorado. David did the cover layout, the formatting and layout of the manuscript, and the publication of the book in e–book and print formats.

David and Leonore are both much–published authors, with a total of 30 books (both fiction and nonfiction) and many articles and essays to their credit. Almost all of their books are available for purchase on Amazon, Apple, Barnes & Noble, and other online buying sites in both e–book and print formats. A few are in audio format and available from Audible.com.

Leonore's memoir, *Another Chance at Life: A Breast Cancer Survivor's Journey*, is available in both English and Spanish.

For details, please see their websites:
David Dvorkin: www.dvorkin.com
Leonore H. Dvorkin: www.leonoredvorkin.com